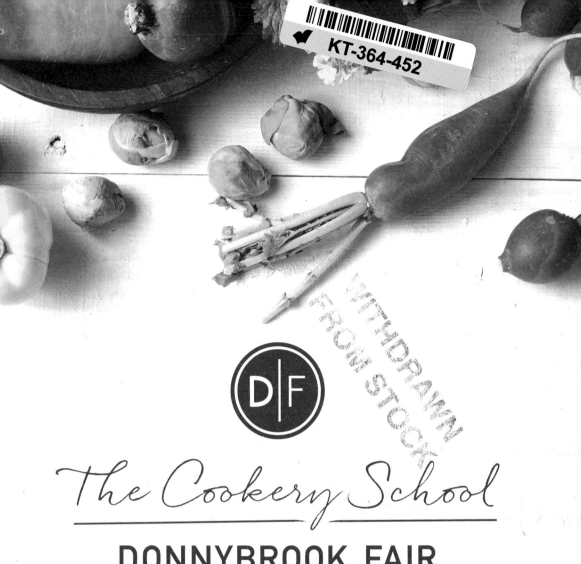

The Cookery School

DONNYBROOK FAIR

NIALL MURPHY

MERCIER PRESS

IRISH PUBLISHER – IRISH STORY

MERCIER PRESS

Cork

www.mercierpress.ie

© Niall Murphy, 2017

Photographed by Rob Kerkvliet – www.afoxinthekitchen.com

Styled by Zita Fox – www.afoxinthekitchen.com

Shutterstock images: pp. 51, 83, 109, 130, 180, 217

ISBN: 978 1 78117 473 9

10 9 8 7 6 5 4 3 2 1

A CIP record for this title is available from the British Library

Printed and bound in the EU.

CONTENTS

Canapés

Stunning Starters

Sensational Salads

Winter & Summer Soups

Cooking Meat to Perfection

Sushi

Vegetable Sides

The Humble Potato

The Art of Sauces

The Great DF Bake Off

Chocolate Heaven

Glorious Desserts

INTRODUCTION

My journey with food has been incredible. There is a saying, somewhere, that if you really love your job then work is easy. I can definitely attest to that, as I really do believe that I have the best job in the world – teaching people how to cook.

From an early age my mum would involve me in cooking and showed great patience as I destroyed the kitchen. It left me with such happy memories, which, in later life, would bring me back to a love of food.

When I left school I knew that I definitely didn't want to go to college. Education and I never had an easy relationship, so I was determined to go straight out into the world. I followed my dad into the motor business. Work afforded me the opportunity to travel extensively around the world, and I came to enjoy exploring different cultures and particularly the food of these places. I found myself collecting local cookbooks wherever I went.

One day, at the height of Recession Ireland, I was driving on the motorway to work when it dawned on me that I was not enjoying what I was doing. It was one of those 'Road to Damascus' moments. I didn't know what I wanted to do, but knew that it was not my current career of twenty-seven years. I left my job soon after.

After a time of reflection I found myself returning to those happy childhood memories of food, and while doing a bit of research I came across a cooking course run by Fáilte Ireland. I completed an application form and two weeks later was called for an interview. I'm not sure what they thought about this fortysomething sitting in front of them, but they took a chance and I was offered a place. The course was sixteen weeks and I loved it. It made me realise that this was what I wanted to do.

At the end of the course, Fáilte Ireland asked me stay on for an extra couple of weeks as they were running a cookery camp for local children. At the end of this they asked if I was interested in going to Leuven in Belgium for six months to continue my training. An interview was arranged and I was offered a place. So off I went, staying in a student house where the average age was nineteen and working in the Institute for Ireland in Europe. I remember coming home after my shift and all my fellow students were in the communal area chatting to each other through social media. My cheery hello was met with an impatient 'log on, man' – truly a mark of the generation gap.

It was in Leuven that I met Ben, the head chef, who is and continues to be a good friend and inspiration to me. Ben was to admit afterwards that he was not too thrilled at the prospect of teaching a student of my advancing years. However, he taught me so much – patience, organisation, traditional and modern cooking techniques – and encouraged me to rethink my relationship with education.

I returned to Dublin and, taking on board Ben's advice and encouragement, I enrolled in the Total Immersion Chef Programme in IT Tallaght. This was a six-month programme where I attended college three days a week while working as a pastry chef at the Portmarnock Links Hotel. It was a long six months but I so enjoyed studying the theory behind the practical skill of cooking. It all made perfect sense.

Shortly after I graduated from ITT my cousin, Brian, asked Ben and I to cater his fiftieth birthday. He wanted a taster menu for thirty-six guests in his beautiful home and requested all the ingredients be sourced from Donnybrook Fair. Ben and I arrived on site to select ingredients, and wandered into a wine tasting in the restaurant. When a gentleman sat down beside me I discovered he was Joe Doyle, the managing director of Donnybrook Fair. We spoke and he seemed fascinated by my journey. We parted company but some weeks later Joe rang me. He had tracked me down through my cousin and asked to meet.

We sat in the restaurant over a coffee and he told me about the Donnybrook Fair Cookery School next door. He was looking for someone with both a knowledge of food and business to manage the school, and thought that I would be a perfect fit. He brought me into the school and I fell in love with the place immediately. It took me all of three minutes to accept. A couple of weeks later I was preparing for my first class.

Today, almost six years later, I am still here. I thoroughly enjoy the demonstration and hands-on classes we do for adults; the teambuilding events; the many guest celebrity chefs who visit the school; and I particularly enjoy the classes we run for children. It is such a gift to share the experience of food with children, as my mum did with me when I was their age.

I returned once again to college to complete a degree in Culinary Arts and Food Science at ITT and have just graduated from DIT with a Masters in Culinary Innovation and New Product Development. As you can see, my relationship with education has reached a whole new level. It's never too late. The college experience has been amazing and I have achieved goals that I never thought possible.

So, at last I have the opportunity to write my first cookbook. I thought long and hard about what this book should be about. Finally I decided that it must be true to the ethos on which the Donnybrook Fair Cookery School is based: simple food really well done. Translations of Ancient Greek texts attribute the following quotation to Hippocrates: 'Let food be thy medicine and medicine be thy food'. With this statement the Ancient Greeks firmly established the link between health and diet. A more modern interpretation of this quote is that 'we are what we eat'. One of the most important things I have learned on my education journey is that when we cook for ourselves we control the sugars, salts and food additives in our diet. This book is not setting out to teach you anything new. What I hope to accomplish is to encourage you to cook simple recipes, with great ingredients, that cover a wide variety of cooking techniques. I also want to take some of the mystery out of cooking, and give you an insight into my world, a world where simple food, brilliantly done, is unbeatable.

I hope you enjoy the recipes in this book and know the joy it brings me sharing my world of food with you.

Niall

TOP TIPS FOR SUCCESSFUL COOKING

▶ Simple food, brilliantly done, is unbeatable. Often we get very ambitious and this can cause stress when we cook for others, which, in turn, can cause things to go wrong. Cooking should be a very relaxed and fun activity. If you are having friends round it is a good idea to practise the dish first.

▶ Plan ahead. Make sure you have all the ingredients and equipment before you start.

▶ Read the recipe and methods carefully before you start so that you are familiar with the recipe and what you have to do.

▶ Follow the recipe exactly. Only when you have mastered the recipe can you experiment and change it to your own tastes.

▶ Be focused and block out any distractions going on around you, e.g. mobile phones, TV, people trying to chat to you.

▶ Always use the best-quality ingredients that you can, as this has a dramatic effect on the final result.

▶ Be very organised. Gather all your ingredients, weigh and measure them, prepare and chop everything before you start to mix and cook. You will often hear the phrase 'mise en place' on cookery programmes. This translates as everything in its place before you start. Have all your prepared ingredients laid out in front of you.

▶ Invest in good kitchen equipment. Look after your equipment and it will last for a very long time.

▶ Clean as you go, keeping your work surfaces clean, as cluttered spaces create stress when you can't find an ingredient or somewhere to place a hot tray coming out of the oven.

▶ Keep a very close eye on food as it cooks; home ovens vary quite a bit so dishes may take a longer or shorter time than the recipe states. Where a recipe just gives you a temperature and makes no reference to a fan oven, then the instructions are for a non-fan oven. If you have a fan oven, adjust the temperature down by 20°C.

- ▶ Write on your cookbooks. Make small notes of things that strike you so that you can remember it next time you make the recipe. I often have students at the school telling me they made an amazing adaptation to one of our recipes but were not able to recreate the dish as they had forgotten what they had done.

- ▶ When adding herbs to a dish at the end of cooking, or to garnish, it is important that you only use the leaves as the stalks can be bitter. Also, only chop the herbs at the last minute as otherwise they will deteriorate on the board very quickly.

- ▶ Always rest your meat after cooking for at least half the time that it was cooked. The meat should be rested on a wooden board, covered in a layer of baking parchment, tinfoil and then a clean tea towel. Leave to rest in a warm place. I use my top oven for this. Resting allows all the juices to redistribute throughout the meat and ensure a tender result.

- ▶ Many of us do not have the time to make our own stocks. Remember to buy only the best quality stock cubes or stock pots. Keep a close eye on the labelling as some of them have a very high salt content.

- ▶ Store your ingredients in the same conditions as you purchased them. If you change the storage conditions they will deteriorate much faster.

RECOMMENDED LIST OF KITCHEN EQUIPMENT

- ▶ Large chopping boards that give you plenty of space to prepare. Always place a damp tea towel under your board to stop it from slipping when you chop.

- ▶ Good-quality knives. These do not have to be expensive – just make sure when you are investing in them that you hold them before you make the purchase. The knife should feel comfortable in your hand. Too heavy and your arm will get tired chopping, too light and the same happens as you have to put extra effort into the chopping. Look after your knives well. Hand wash only and store in a drawer wrapped in a tea towel. Sharpen your knives every day.

- ▶ Heavy, all-metal, non-stick frying pans. The heat conducts very well in a heavy pan and makes it easier to cook to perfection and not burn food. The all-metal ones are fantastic as you can put them into the oven when required. Also good-quality, heavy casserole pots.

- ▶ Heatproof spatulas. These are the new wooden spoon as they are much easier to work with, do not transfer flavours as wooden spoons do and are much easier to wash.

- ▶ A food processor. Makes very light work of chopping, grating and mixing.

- ▶ A hand blender. Much easier to blend soups in the pot rather than trying to transfer to a food blender.

- ▶ A food mixer with a stand is very useful. It means that you always have two hands free rather than trying to balance with one hand and add ingredients with the other.

- ▶ A good-quality vegetable peeler. Also a julienne peeler for salads.

- ▶ A large selection of small bowls for your mise en place.

- A wet and dry spice grinder is essential. These are inexpensive to buy but are brilliant for making not only curry pastes but also for emulsifying salad dressings.

- A micro-plane. These are fine graters and I use them a lot for preparing garlic and ginger.

- Heavy-duty oven gloves or dry tea towels. It is never a good idea to take hot trays from the oven with a damp or wet tea towel – this will conduct heat at an alarming rate and burn you very easily.

- Finally, my number one kitchen gadget is an instant-read food thermometer. This can be sourced from any good kitchen shop or online and enables you to cook meat to perfection, ensuring that it is never under- or over-cooked. See overleaf for how these thermometers work and the important temperatures.

INSTANT-READ FOOD THERMOMETER

Some of you may remember, or still have, a meat thermometer in your drawer at home. This was a disc-shaped temperature gauge with a spike that was inserted into the meat to check its core temperature. They worked but were slow and cumbersome to use. Today we have a range of digital food thermometers, which do the same job but in a much faster and easier way.

We often see chefs on TV pressing on meat to learn how far the cooking process has gone. During our hands-on classes in the school, I find that students have difficulty translating touch to temperature – particularly at first – and so I highly recommend an instant-read food thermometer.

The probe is inserted into the middle of the meat or fish to check if it has cooked correctly. The important thing to remember is to check the part of the meat or fish where the heat takes longest to penetrate. For beef, pork and fish this is very easy to access. With a roast chicken, this is not so easy. To check the core cooking temperature of a whole chicken insert the probe into the centre of the breast first (the thickest part away from the carcass) but then also double-check by inserting it in the inner thigh.

As a general guide all minced meats, burgers, sausages, etc. must be cooked to a core temperature of 75°C. All chicken and pork products must also be cooked to a core temperature of 75°C. Products such as beef and lamb, when not minced, can be cooked to lower temperatures: rare, medium rare, medium and well done.

The chart opposite gives you a guide for the recipes contained in this book, as well as for cooking meats that are not in this book but which will be useful to know.

Always remember to rest your meats after cooking. The meat will rise another 1–2 degrees during the resting period.

The food probe will enable you to cook meat to perfection and ensure that you are cooking safely.

PRODUCT	LEVEL COOKED	INTERNAL CORE TEMPERATURE
Beef/ Lamb	Rare Medium Rare Medium Medium Well Well	50°C 55°C 60°C 65°C Above 70°C
Chicken/ Whole Duck	Well	75°C
Pork	Well	75°C
Minced Meat/ Sausages/Burgers	Well	75°C
Turkey	Well	75°C
Fish/Seafood	Perfectly	55°C

Great Start Breakfasts

SERVES 12

ORANGE & MIXED FRUIT GRANOLA

This is always the first recipe we do when we run our Transition Year and children's camps here at the cookery school. It's a great breakfast cereal, full of flavour and packed with all the right things. It also stores really well in an airtight container.

INGREDIENTS

200ml 100% pure maple syrup

zest of 2 oranges

3 tbsp water

2 tbsp coconut oil

2 tbsp sunflower oil

pinch of salt

300g rolled oats

200g mixed seeds (linseeds, sunflower seeds, sesame seeds, pumpkin seeds)

100g Donnybrook Fair luxury nut mix, roughly chopped (pistachios, almonds, walnuts and pecans)

200g mixed dried fruits (sultanas, cherries, blueberries, cranberries)

Preheat the oven to 170°C/150°C fan/gas mark 3. Line a large baking tray with non-stick baking paper.

On a low heat, gently heat the maple syrup, orange zest, water, coconut oil, sunflower oil and salt together. Heat until the coconut oil has melted. Do not boil.

In a large bowl, combine the oats, seeds and nuts. Pour the warmed liquid over them and mix well.

Spread this mix onto the lined baking tray. Bake in the oven for 20 minutes, stir through and cook for another 20 minutes. Continue this process until all the granola is a golden-brown. Depending on how big your tray is and the depth of the mix, this may take three or four rotations.

Remove from the oven and allow to cool for about 30 minutes. Stir in the dried fruits and store in an airtight container.

SERVES 4

SCRAMBLED EGGS WITH SMOKED SALMON

Making beautifully soft scrambled eggs is an exercise in time and patience, but it's definitely worth the effort. I serve this on slices of toasted sourdough. This dish is also fantastic with crispy bacon instead of the salmon. It's best not to season the eggs until after they are cooked. It's also important that you don't overcook them.

INGREDIENTS

25g butter

6 large eggs

2 tbsp cream

salt and freshly ground black pepper

4 slices of toasted sourdough bread

60g thinly sliced Donnybrook Fair smoked salmon

Place a pan on a medium heat and melt the butter.

Whisk the eggs gently in a bowl until they are well mixed, then add to the pan. Stir gently for 2–3 minutes, until the eggs are cooked to your liking. The eggs should be soft and slightly runny.

Remove the pan from the heat and stir in the cream. Season with salt and pepper.

Place the soft scrambled eggs on the toasted sourdough, gently place the smoked salmon on top and give a final turn of the pepper mill over the top.

REHYDRATED MANGO YOGURT

For this recipe I use a Donnybrook Fair mango smoothie, but you can use any flavoured good-quality smoothie or juice to create a variety of rehydrated yogurts.

INGREDIENTS

500g full-fat natural yogurt

100ml Donnybrook Fair mango smoothie

1 tbsp maple syrup

1 tsp vanilla extract

1 small ripe mango, peeled and diced

Place a sieve lined with muslin over a bowl. Add the yogurt to the muslin-lined sieve and leave in the fridge to drain overnight so that as much moisture as possible will be removed.

Place the strained yogurt into a bowl and stir in the mango smoothie, maple syrup and vanilla. Add the diced fresh mango and serve.

MAKES
12

AMERICAN PANCAKES WITH MAPLE SYRUP

Maple syrup is a fantastic unrefined natural sweetener to use. However, make sure that the label clearly states that it's 100% pure maple syrup. For a variation on these pancakes, when the batter is in the pan you can add some fresh blueberries or raspberries before you flip them over.

INGREDIENTS

225g self-raising flour

1 tsp baking powder

pinch of salt

25g butter

2 large eggs

300ml milk

vegetable oil

To serve:

fresh berries

maple syrup

Sift the flour, baking powder and salt into a large bowl.

Melt the butter in a small pan over a low heat. Allow the butter to cool a little once it has melted.

Beat the eggs and milk together in a medium bowl, then gently stir into the flour mix. Stir in the cooled melted butter.

Heat a heavy-based non-stick pan on a medium heat. Lightly brush the pan with oil.

Add a large tablespoon of batter to the pan and shape into a circle. Repeat to make a few more pancakes, but don't overcrowd the pan.

After 3–4 minutes, when you see bubbles appear on the surface of the pancake, gently flip it over. The pancake should be golden and puffed on its now upturned side. Cook on the other side for a further 3 minutes, then transfer to a plate and keep warm in a low oven.

Wipe the pan with some kitchen paper and repeat the process.

Serve with some fresh berries and maple syrup.

MAKES
4

MANGO & ORANGE GRANOLA POTS

These breakfast pots are a combination of the previous recipes. This shows how you can take different ingredients and present them in other ways to create a new breakfast dish.

INGREDIENTS

16 tbsp rehydrated mango yogurt (page 27)

8 tbsp orange and mixed fruit granola (page 22)

1 ripe mango, peeled and sliced

Place 1½ tablespoons of the rehydrated mango yogurt in a serving glass, then add 1 tablespoon of the granola. Repeat the process to create two layers.

Place 1 tablespoon of yogurt on top of the granola and garnish with some fresh mango slices.

MAKES
4

CHILLED QUINOA PORRIDGE

This is a filling cereal and is perhaps my favourite summer breakfast cereal. I especially like how you can use different fruits, both dried and fresh, as well as nuts to liven up the recipe.

INGREDIENTS

120g quinoa flakes

350ml full-fat milk

120ml water

60g assorted Donnybrook Fair shelled nut mix (pistachio, almonds, walnuts, cashew)

100g natural yogurt

1 tbsp maple syrup

1 Granny Smith apple

1 ripe Conference pear

1 tsp ground cinnamon

Place the quinoa flakes, milk and water in a small pot with a lid. Bring to the boil, stirring all the time. Reduce the heat to a simmer and cook for 10–15 minutes with the lid on until the quinoa is cooked. Remove from the heat, remove the lid and allow to cool completely.

Preheat the oven to 220°C/200°C fan/gas mark 7. Line a baking tray with non-stick baking paper.

Scatter the nuts in the lined tray in an even layer. Roast the nuts in the oven for 5–10 minutes, watching them carefully to ensure they don't burn. They will take on a light colour and release a wonderful nut aroma when ready. Remove from the oven and allow to cool, then roughly chop.

Place the cooled quinoa flakes in a bowl and stir in the yogurt and maple syrup.

Coarsely grate the apple and the pear, with the skin on, into the bowl, then add the chopped nuts and cinnamon to taste. Add more yogurt or milk if you prefer a looser texture.

The Art of
Bread Making

BROWN BREAD WITH TREACLE

One of my favourite classes at the cookery school is the 'Art of Bread Making' class. I thoroughly enjoy the wonderful sense of satisfaction as students head home clutching a wide variety of breads that they have made. This is a no-nonsense bread that is quick to make. The milk and treacle create a bread rich in flavour and beautifully moist. To make a Guinness version, just split the buttermilk portion to half buttermilk and half Guinness and follow the steps as below.

INGREDIENTS

sunflower oil

225g plain flour

1 tsp salt

1 tsp baking powder

1 tsp bicarbonate of soda

150g wholemeal flour

75g coarse wholemeal flour

25g cold butter, cubed

30g rich dark brown sugar

350ml buttermilk

1 tbsp treacle

handful of porridge oats

Preheat the oven to 220°C/200°C fan/gas mark 7. Lightly oil a 1lb bread tin with sunflower oil.

Sift the plain flour, salt, baking powder and bicarbonate of soda into a large bowl. Add the wholemeal flours and mix well. Rub the butter gently into the flour with your fingertips to achieve a breadcrumb texture. Add the sugar and mix well.

Place the buttermilk and treacle in a pan and heat gently to dissolve the treacle into the buttermilk. Add the warm buttermilk into the dry ingredients and stir well to make sure the dough is mixed and there are no flour pockets. Transfer to the oiled tin and sprinkle the top with the oats.

Place in the oven and bake for 15 minutes. Reduce the heat to 200°C/180°C fan/gas mark 6 and bake for 30 minutes. Remove the bread from the tin and return to the oven for 5 minutes.

Remove the bread from the oven and allow it to cool on a wire rack. Once cooled, you can enjoy this wonderful bread sliced and spread with butter and marmalade. It's equally good with smoked salmon.

EASY SOURDOUGH BREAD

I love sourdough bread, but much like indoor plants, I have never been able to look after a sourdough starter for any length of time. My excuse is that I'm too busy teaching! This recipe is the easiest sourdough bread to make and, best of all, it requires no kneading.

INGREDIENTS

600g strong white flour, plus extra for dusting

2 tsp salt

50g rye flour

50g wholemeal flour

7g fast action dried yeast or 15g fresh yeast

600ml warm water

Sift the strong white flour and salt into a large bowl, then add the rye and wholemeal flours and stir well. Add the dried yeast and mix well. (If using fresh yeast do not add here – crumble it into the warm water and rest for 10 minutes before adding.)

Make a well in the centre of the dry ingredients, then stir in the warm water and mix until everything is combined, but make sure you don't mix for too long. The dough should be wet and sticky.

Cover the bowl with cling film and leave in a cool (but not cold) place for 18 hours.

Preheat the oven to 230°C/210°C fan/gas mark 8. Heat a large, heavy-based casserole with the lid on for at least 15 minutes in the oven.

Remove the pot from the oven, sprinkle the base with some strong white flour, then pour in the dough.

Bake in the oven with the lid on for 40 minutes. Remove the lid and bake for a further 20 minutes.

Tip the bread out of the casserole and tap the bottom: it should sound hollow when it's baked. Cool on a wire rack before slicing.

WHITE YEAST BREAD PLAIT

As with the sourdough bread on page 35, if you can get fresh yeast you will achieve a better flavour in your bread, but as this can be difficult to find, there are a variety of fast-acting yeast brands that work really well.

INGREDIENTS

500g strong white bread flour, plus extra for dusting

7g fast action dried yeast or 15g fresh yeast

2 tsp salt

1 tsp sugar

300ml warm water

2 tbsp olive oil

1 egg, beaten with 1 tsp water for the egg wash

Tip the flour into a mixing bowl. If using fast action dried yeast, stir this into the flour. If using fresh yeast crumble it into the warm water and rest for 10 minutes. Add the salt and sugar to the flour.

Make a well in the centre of the dry ingredients. Pour in the warm water all at once and 1 tablespoon of oil. Mix quickly using your hands to make a soft and slightly sticky dough.

Sprinkle the work surface with a little flour and tip out the dough. (Use just enough flour on the surface to stop your dough from sticking.) Knead by stretching it away from you, then folding it in half towards you and pushing it away with the heel of your hand. Knead for 10–15 minutes, until the dough is smooth and stretchable.

When the dough is smooth and stretchable, roll it into a ball and put it into a large, clean bowl. Cover the bowl with cling film and leave for 1 hour in a warm, draught-free place, until it has doubled in size. The dough is ready once it springs back when you press it gently with your finger.

Tip the dough onto a floured surface, give it a quick knead and shape it into a long fat cylinder. With the dough facing lengthwise away from you, cut two incisions from the bottom to the top. Make sure not to cut all the way to the end, however. These incisions are done simply to create three even sausage shapes that form the strands of the plait.

Plait the three strands, bringing the outside left strand over the middle strand, then the right strand over the middle. Continue all the way to the bottom and tuck the ends of the strands under the bread and pinch to hold them together.

Place on a baking sheet oiled with a tablespoon of oil, cover loosely with cling film and leave for a second rise for 30 minutes.

Preheat the oven to 230°C/210°C fan/gas mark 8.

Brush the top of the plait with a little egg wash and bake in the oven for 30–35 minutes, until browned and crisp. Cool on a wire rack.

SERVES
10-12

BLUE CHEESE & CARAMELISED ONION FOCACCIA

Focaccia is a classic Italian bread. Once the basic dough is made, however, you can be really creative with the flavours and textures. This version of the recipe is by far my favourite, but for a simpler bread you can just scatter the dough with finely chopped fresh rosemary and garlic.

INGREDIENTS

500g strong white flour, plus extra for dusting

1 tsp salt

7g fast action dried yeast

350ml warm water

olive oil

1 portion of caramelised onions (page 212)

150g blue cheese, crumbled

1 tsp flaked sea salt

Sift the flour and salt into a large bowl, then mix the yeast into the flour. Add the warm water and mix until you have a soft dough.

Sprinkle the work surface with a little flour and tip out the dough. (Use just enough flour on the surface to stop your dough from sticking.) Knead by stretching it away from you, then folding it in half towards you and pushing it away with the heel of your hand. Knead for 10–15 minutes, until the dough is smooth and stretchable.

Lightly oil a clean bowl with olive oil. Roll the dough into a ball and place it in the lightly oiled bowl, cover with cling film and leave to rise for 1 hour in a warm, draught-free place, until it has doubled in size.

After 1 hour, place the dough into a 37 x 27cm baking tray lined with non-stick baking paper. Flatten the dough out into a rectangular shape, then gently roll with a rolling pin to ensure it is even. Drizzle with olive oil and top with the caramelised onions, blue cheese and sea salt.

Cover loosely with cling film and leave to rest again for another 30 minutes.

Preheat the oven to 230°C/210°C fan/gas mark 8.

Bake the focaccia in the oven for about 15 minutes, until evenly golden-brown. Once cooked, remove the bread from the oven and take it out of the tin. It should sound hollow when you tap the base. Immediately drizzle some olive oil all over the top. Leave to cool on a wire rack, then cut into squares and serve.

CHERRY & VANILLA SCONES

I use yogurt for this recipe instead of the traditional buttermilk. This gives a much softer texture to the scone. To create a savoury scone, replace the vanilla yogurt with plain yogurt and the cherries with coarsely grated Cheddar and some chopped fresh chives.

INGREDIENTS

250g self-raising flour

small pinch of salt

40g cold butter, cut into small cubes

75g glacé cherries

about 375ml vanilla yogurt

1 egg, beaten with a splash of water, to glaze

Preheat the oven to 230°C/210°C fan/gas mark 8.

Sift the flour and salt into a large bowl and mix together. Using your fingertips, rub in the butter until you have a fine breadcrumb texture. Add the cherries whole.

Make a well in the centre. Stirring gently with a fork, add enough of the yogurt into the dry ingredients to create a soft dough, adding more yogurt if necessary. The dough should be soft but not sticky.

Turn out the dough onto a lightly floured work surface and gently shape into a rectangle that's 4–5cm thick. Cut the dough into eight even rectangles and place on a baking tray. Brush the top of the scones with the beaten egg.

Bake in the centre of the oven for 10–15 minutes, until golden-brown on top. Cool on a wire rack. Serve split in half and spread with butter.

MAKES 2 LOAVES

WHOLEGRAIN SPELT BREAD

This bread does contain a small amount of gluten, so it's not suitable for coeliacs. Warming the milk for this recipe serves two purposes: firstly to dissolve the treacle, and secondly, the warm liquid is absorbed much faster and easier by the flour.

INGREDIENTS

475g wholegrain spelt flour

1 tsp baking powder

1 tsp bicarbonate of soda

1 tsp fine sea salt

150g mixed seeds (sunflower, pumpkin, linseeds, etc.)

50g sultanas

550ml buttermilk, warmed

1 tbsp treacle

Preheat the oven to 180°C/160°C fan/gas mark 4. Line two 1lb loaf tins with non-stick baking paper.

Sift the flour, baking powder, bicarbonate of soda and sea salt into a large bowl, then stir in the mixed seeds and sultanas.

Place the buttermilk and treacle in a pan and gently warm on a low heat to dissolve the treacle. Be careful not to overheat the buttermilk. Make a well in the centre of the dry ingredients, then add the liquid, mixing together until combined.

Pour the dough into the lined loaf tins and bake in the oven for 1 hour, until well risen.

Remove from the oven, gently remove the loaves from the tins and place directly on the wire shelves in the oven for a further 5 minutes to ensure a crisp crust.

Remove from the oven and cool on a wire rack before slicing.

Jams &
Chutneys

STRAWBERRY VANILLA JAM

The taste of your own homemade jam is really unbeatable. I'm a massive fan of vanilla and find any excuse to use it, and I think it brings this jam to a new level.

INGREDIENTS

1kg fresh strawberries, hulled and chopped if too big

1 large vanilla pod, cut in half lengthways

1kg jam sugar

juice of 1 lemon

The night before, place the strawberries, the halved vanilla pod and half of the jam sugar in a large plastic or ceramic bowl. Stir well and cover with cling film. Leave in a cool place overnight.

The following day, place the strawberry mix in a wide stainless steel saucepan. Add the remaining jam sugar and the lemon juice. Stir well and attach a sugar thermometer to the side of the pan. Bring the mix to a rapid boil until it reaches setting point, 105°C. While the jam is boiling, remove any froth that gathers on the top of the jam.

Alternatively, if you don't have a sugar thermometer, to test if the jam has reached setting point, place a small plate in the freezer for 15 minutes. Remove the plate from the freezer and remove the jam from the heat, then place a spoonful of the hot jam on the cold plate. Once the jam has cooled, push your finger through the jam to form a line. If the setting point has been reached, the surface of the jam should wrinkle and the jam should not refill the line you have created. If the jam does refill the line, return the pan to the heat and cook for a further 5 minutes, then repeat the wrinkle test.

Remove the vanilla pod, scrape out any seeds and stir them through the jam. Leave the jam to sit for 30 minutes, then remove any froth that has settled on the top of the jam.

Preheat the oven to 140°C/120°C fan/gas mark 1 as the jam sits.

Wash your jars in hot soapy water, rinse them really well and transfer to the oven, placing them directly on the wire rack for 30 minutes. This will sterilise the jars.

Stir the jam well, then ladle it into the jars. Once full, place a waxed disc on top of each jar and immediately seal with cellophane lids. Store in a cool dark place for up to a year. Once opened, store in the fridge for up to one month.

MAKES
APPROX.
500G

LEMON CURD

You can't beat the flavour and texture of homemade curds. Lemon curd is a great one to start with, as once you have mastered the technique you can get creative with lime, raspberry, strawberry and blackberry curd.

INGREDIENTS

zest and juice of 4 unwaxed lemons

200g caster sugar

100g unsalted butter, cut into small cubes, at room temperature

3 large eggs

1 egg yolk

Preheat the oven to 140°C/120°C fan/gas mark 1.

Wash your jars in hot soapy water, rinse them really well and transfer to the oven, placing them directly on the wire rack for 30 minutes. This will sterilise the jars.

Place the lemon zest and juice in a heatproof glass bowl. Add the other ingredients to the bowl and whisk until all are mixed well.

Place the bowl over a pan of barely simmering water. This is called a bain marie. Make sure that the bottom of the bowl is not touching the water, as this will cause the eggs to overheat and curdle. Whisk as the mixture heats and thickens to the desired consistency, then remove from the heat.

Ladle the lemon curd into the sterilised jars. Once full, place a waxed disc on top of each jar and immediately seal with cellophane lids. Store in the fridge, unopened, for up to three months. Once opened, keep in the fridge and use within one week.

MAKES
APPROX.
2KG

RHUBARB & GINGER JAM

One of the best times here in the cookery school is when students drop in with homegrown produce. Rhubarb is very popular, so I get a lot of rhubarb throughout the season. This a great recipe to make use of this abundant crop.

INGREDIENTS

1.8kg rhubarb, trimmed

1.8kg granulated sugar

zest and juice of 2 unwaxed
  lemons

25–50g fresh ginger, peeled

50g preserved stem ginger in
  syrup, chopped

Wash the rhubarb and cut into 2.5cm pieces. Put in a large bowl with the sugar and the lemon zest and juice. Leave to stand overnight.

The next day, put the rhubarb mix into a wide stainless steel saucepan and attach a sugar thermometer to the side.

Place the peeled ginger on a chopping board and tap it with a rolling pin to flatten it slightly. Tie up the bruised ginger in a clean muslin bag and add to the pan. Stir continuously over a low heat until the sugar has dissolved.

Increase the heat to high and boil rapidly until you reach the setting point, 105°C. While the jam is boiling, remove any froth that gathers on the top of the jam.

Alternatively, if you don't have a sugar thermometer, to test if the jam has reached setting point, place a small plate in the freezer for 15 minutes. Remove the plate from the freezer and remove the jam from the heat, then place a spoonful of the hot jam on the cold plate. Once the jam has cooled, push your finger through the jam to form a line. If the setting point has been reached, the surface of the jam should wrinkle and the jam should not refill the line you have created. If the jam does refill the line, return the pan to the heat and cook for a further 5 minutes, then repeat the wrinkle test.

Remove from the heat and stir in the chopped stem ginger. Remove the bag of fresh ginger, then leave to rest for 30 minutes. Remove any froth that has settled on the top of the jam.

Preheat the oven to 140°C/120°C fan/gas mark 1 as the jam sits.

Wash your jars in hot soapy water, rinse them really well and transfer to the oven, placing them directly on the wire rack for 30 minutes. This will sterilise the jars.

Stir the jam well, then ladle it into the jars. Once full, place a waxed disc on top of each jar and immediately seal with cellophane lids. Store in a cool dark place for up to a year. Once opened, store in the fridge for up to one month.

MAKES APPROX. 1.5KG

THREE FRUIT MARMALADE

Homemade bread and marmalade is a match made in heaven. In making this marmalade you will use a technique called the 'whole fruit method'. This means that you are using all of the fruit. Leaving everything in, even the pith, adds to the flavour.

INGREDIENTS

2 oranges

1 pink grapefruit

1 lemon

1kg granulated sugar

Wash the fruit well and place in a large pot with a tight-fitting lid. Cover with water and place on a high heat. The fruit will float, but you just need to make sure that the fruit is well covered when you push the fruit to the bottom of the pan.

Bring the water to the boil, then reduce the heat, place the lid on and simmer until the fruit is soft. This should take 1½–2 hours. Keep an eye on the pot to make sure it doesn't boil dry. Add a little extra water if necessary.

After 1½ hours, test the fruit. It should be very soft. If not, cook for a further 30 minutes. When the fruit is soft, remove the pot from the heat. Leave the water in the pot. There should be about 150–200ml of water left in the pot.

Place the fruit on a board set in a high-sided baking tray to catch any juices that leak out of the fruit.

When the fruit is cool enough to handle, cut it in half and scrape out all the flesh. Add the flesh to the water in the pot. Slice the rind, including the pith, to your preferred thickness and add it to the pot. Pour any juices in the tray into the pan too. Add the sugar and stir well.

Place the pot on a low heat and stir until the sugar has dissolved. Attach a sugar thermometer to the side of the pot, then bring to the boil and boil until you reach the setting point, 105°C. While the jam is boiling, remove any froth that gathers on the top of the marmalade.

Alternatively, if you don't have a sugar thermometer, to test if the jam has reached setting point, place a small plate in the freezer for 15 minutes. Remove the plate from the freezer and remove the jam from the heat, then place a spoonful of the hot jam on the cold plate. Once the jam has cooled, push your finger through the jam to form a line. If the setting point has been reached, the surface of the jam should wrinkle and the jam should not refill the line you have created. If the jam does refill the line, return the pan to the heat and cook for a further 5 minutes, then repeat the wrinkle test.

Remove from the heat and allow it to sit for 30 minutes, then remove any froth that has settled on the top of the marmalade.

Preheat the oven to 140°C/120°C fan/gas mark 1 as the marmalade sits.

Wash your jars in hot soapy water, rinse them really well and transfer to the oven, placing them directly on the wire rack for 30 minutes. This will sterilise the jars.

Stir the marmalade well, then ladle it into the jars. Once full, place a waxed disc on top of each jar and immediately seal with cellophane lids. Store in a cool dark place for up to a year. Once opened, store in the fridge for up to one month.

KUMQUAT & PEAR CHUTNEY

The Irish don't eat a lot of chutneys, but we really should. This recipe goes brilliantly with cold meats and is a great addition to any cheeseboard.

INGREDIENTS

250g caster sugar

3 tbsp water

150g kumquats, halved and seeded

1 red onion, finely diced

3 pears, skin on, cored and diced

180ml cider vinegar

4 green cardamom pods

2 cloves

1 cinnamon stick

2 tsp salt

1 tsp ground allspice

½ tsp chilli flakes

Place the sugar and water in a non-stick saucepan with a tight-fitting lid. Have a bowl of cold water and a pastry brush beside you at the hob. Set the pan over a low heat and allow the sugar to dissolve – do not stir.

When the sugar has dissolved, turn up the heat to medium and allow the syrup to boil until it turns a light golden caramel colour. Every minute or so, brush the inside of the pan with some cold water just above the line of the sugar and water to dissolve any splashes from the sugar syrup. Watch carefully, as it will caramelise very quickly. This should take about 10 minutes. Take the pan off the heat as soon as it has turned that light golden colour.

Add the kumquats and onion. The caramel will harden, but don't worry. Add the rest of the ingredients and return the pan to a low heat. Gently stir to allow the caramel to melt and mix well.

Increase the heat to high and bring to the boil, then reduce the heat and simmer with the lid on for 30 minutes, stirring occasionally to stop the syrup from catching.

Remove the lid and simmer for a further 30 minutes. The liquid should reduce by half and the mix should thicken during this period. Remove from the heat and allow to sit for a further 30 minutes, then remove any froth that has settled on the top of the chutney.

Preheat the oven to 140°C/120°C fan/gas mark 1 as the chutney sits.

Wash your jars in hot soapy water, rinse them really well and transfer to the oven, placing them directly on the wire rack for 30 minutes. This will sterilise the jars.

Remove the cardamom pods from the chutney, stir it well and ladle it into the jars. Once full, place a waxed disc on top of each jar and immediately seal with cellophane lids. Store in a cool dark place for up to a year. Once opened, store in the fridge for up to two weeks.

MAKES APPROX. 1.5KG

MANGO CHUTNEY

This chutney goes really well with cold meats and cheeses. It's also a great addition to any Indian food.

INGREDIENTS

3 large ripe mangos

2 tbsp sunflower oil

2 onions, halved and thinly sliced

thumb-sized piece of fresh ginger, peeled and cut into thin shreds

10 green cardamom pods

1 cinnamon stick

½ tsp cumin seeds

½ tsp coriander seeds, lightly crushed

¼ tsp black onion seeds

½ tsp ground turmeric

2 cooking apples, peeled, cored and chopped

500ml water

1 large red chilli, deseeded and finely sliced

375ml white wine vinegar

400g caster sugar

1 tsp salt

Cut each mango in half down the sides of the flat stone that runs through the centre of the fruit so that you end up with two fleshy halves. Take one half of the mango and make four parallel cuts through the flesh down to the skin. Make sure you don't cut through the skin. Turn the mango a quarter of a turn and cut four parallel cuts through the flesh down to the skin, but again not through the skin. Now push the mango from the skin side to turn it inside out and slice away the chunks of mango flesh that stand out of the skin. Discard the skin and repeat the process for the other halves. Trim the flesh from around the stones.

Place a pot with a tight-fitting lid on a medium heat and add the oil. When the oil is hot, add the onions and fry them for a few minutes, until they start to soften. Stir in the ginger and cook, stirring frequently, for 8–10 minutes, until the onion is golden. Stir in all the spices except the turmeric and fry for 1 minute, until toasted.

Stir in the turmeric, then add the apples and pour in the water. Cover the pan and cook for 10 minutes. Stir in the mangos and chilli, then cover again and cook for 20 minutes more, until the apple is pulpy and the mango is tender.

Pour in the vinegar and stir in the sugar and salt, then leave to simmer, uncovered, for 30 minutes, stirring frequently (especially towards the end of the cooking time so that it doesn't stick), until the chutney has thickened. Remove from the heat and leave to rest for

30 minutes, then remove any froth that has settled on the top of the chutney.

Preheat the oven to 140°C/120°C fan/gas mark 1 as the chutney sits.

Wash your jars in hot soapy water, rinse them really well and transfer to the oven, placing them directly on the wire rack for 30 minutes. This will sterilise the jars.

Stir the chutney well, then remove the cardamom pods and ladle it into the jars. Once full, place a waxed disc on top of each jar and immediately seal with cellophane lids. Store in a cool dark place for up to a year. Once opened, store in the fridge for up to two weeks.

Welcome Drinks

Making your guests feel very welcome is a cornerstone of what we do here at the cookery school in Donnybrook Fair. There is nothing more welcoming for your guests than to have a special drink ready on arrival. Here are five of my most popular welcome drinks. All the cordials can be diluted with Prosecco, Cava, white lemonade, still or sparkling water, and served with freshly chopped mint leaves and ice.

ORANGE & LEMON CORDIAL

INGREDIENTS

2 lemons

1 orange

150g caster sugar

300ml water

Squeeze the lemons and orange and set the juice aside.

Place the sugar and water in a pot, bring to the boil and boil for 2 minutes. Take the pot off the heat, add the juice and allow to cool. Pass the cordial through a fine sieve and chill until required.

Pour the cordial into a large glass jug and add approximately 1 litre of still or sparkling water, Prosecco, Cava or white lemonade and plenty of ice.

ORANGE & RASPBERRY CORDIAL

INGREDIENTS

3 punnets fresh raspberries

1 orange, sliced

150g caster sugar

300ml water

Place the fruit, sugar and water in a pot. Bring to the boil and boil for 2 minutes. Remove from the heat and allow to cool completely. Pass through a fine sieve and chill until required.

Pour the cordial into a large glass jug and add approximately 1 litre of still or sparkling water, Prosecco, Cava or white lemonade and plenty of ice.

GINGER, LEMONGRASS & LIME CORDIAL

INGREDIENTS

150g caster sugar

300ml water

3 stalks of lemongrass, trimmed and roughly chopped

1 dessertspoon peeled and finely grated fresh ginger

100ml fresh lime juice

Gently heat the sugar and water in a saucepan set over a low heat, stirring to dissolve the sugar. Add the lemongrass and ginger and bring to the boil. Turn off the heat and leave to cool with the lid on, then strain through a fine sieve. Stir in the lime juice and chill.

Pour the cordial into a large glass jug and add approximately 1 litre of still or sparkling water, Prosecco, Cava or white lemonade and plenty of ice.

PINK GRAPEFRUIT & LIMEADE

INGREDIENTS

2 pink grapefruit

2 limes

150g caster sugar

300ml water

Juice the grapefruit and limes and set the juice aside.

In a saucepan, bring the sugar and water to the boil and boil for 2 minutes. Turn off the heat, add the juices and leave to cool. Strain through a fine sieve and chill until required.

Pour the cordial into a large glass jug and add approximately 1 litre of still or sparkling water, Prosecco, Cava or white lemonade and plenty of ice.

MAKES 450ML

ELDERFLOWER CORDIAL

This is such a popular drink when the elderflowers are in season. The season is quite short, between May and June of each year. Before you pick the elderflowers, check their aroma. They should smell fresh and pungent, so keep looking if they have an unpleasant aroma. The cordial will taste the same as the aroma.

INGREDIENTS

150g caster sugar

1 lemon, sliced

300ml water

12 elderflower heads, rinsed

Place the sugar, lemon slices and water in a pot and bring to the boil. As it reaches the boiling point, add the elderflowers. Boil for 2 minutes, then remove from the heat and leave to cool completely. Pass through a clean muslin cloth and chill until required.

Pour the cordial into a large glass jug and add approximately 1 litre of still or sparkling water, Prosecco, Cava or white lemonade and plenty of ice.

Canapés

MINI CRAB CAKES

Tinned crab meat with large chunks of white meat makes fantastic crab cakes. I have tried to make these with expensive fresh crab meat and I don't think it gives the same result. You could also substitute the crab meat with tinned salmon or any firm white fish or even chicken. If using uncooked fish or chicken, pulse the meat in a food processor to a finely chopped texture. I serve these with sweet chilli sauce (p. 232).

INGREDIENTS

25g butter

2 tbsp white wine

225g tinned crab meat
(squeeze out as much brine
as possible)

100g fresh white
breadcrumbs

3 spring onions, chopped

2 garlic cloves, finely grated

1 red chilli, deseeded and
very finely chopped

½ egg, whisked

2 tbsp chopped fresh
coriander, leaves and stalks

½ tbsp Dijon mustard

coconut oil, for frying

Gently heat the butter and wine in a pan.

Mix together all the other ingredients except the coco-nut oil in a large bowl.

Add enough of the melted butter and wine to bring the mix together so that you can form it into cakes (you may not need all the butter and wine). Form into twelve bite-sized crab cakes and chill for 30–40 minutes.

Preheat the oven to 200°C/180°C fan/gas mark 6.

Heat the coconut oil in a heavy-based pan set over a medium heat and gently fry the crab cakes until they are golden-brown on both sides. Transfer to a baking tray and cook in the oven for 10 minutes, until cooked through.

MAKES 24

PARMESAN SHORTBREAD, PARSLEY PESTO & QUINCE JELLY

This is a very simple canapé and the shortbread can be made in advance and stored in an airtight container.

INGREDIENTS

For the shortbread:

150g plain flour

80g Parmesan cheese, finely grated

100g unsalted butter, cold, cut into small cubes

¼ tsp freshly ground black pepper

For parsley pesto:

30g pine nuts

40g Parmesan cheese, finely grated

30g fresh flat-leaf parsley

2 garlic gloves, grated

75ml rapeseed oil

To serve:

quince jelly, diced

Place all the ingredients for the shortbread in a food processor and pulse until it resembles breadcrumbs. Tip onto a work surface and bring the dough together into a ball. Roll the dough into a cylinder about 3cm in diameter. Wrap tightly in cling film and chill while you make the pesto.

Place a dry pan on a low heat and add the pine nuts. Gently shake the pan until the nuts begin to take on a little colour. Transfer to a cold plate and leave to cool completely.

Place all the ingredients for the pesto into a food processor or spice grinder and blitz. Transfer to a clean bowl and chill until required.

Preheat the oven to 180°C/160°C fan/gas mark 4. Line a baking sheet with non-stick baking paper.

Remove the shortbread dough from the fridge and unwrap it. Cut the cylinder into slices about 1.25cm thick and place on the lined baking tray.

Bake in the oven for 12–15 minutes, until golden. Remove from the oven and allow to cool completely on a wire cooling rack.

To serve, place a small dollop of the pesto in the middle of each Parmesan shortbread biscuit and add a small cube of the diced quince jelly.

MAKES
16

CHEESE PUFFS

This is the same method as making choux pastry. You may not need to add all the egg, so follow the instructions carefully.

INGREDIENTS

40g unsalted butter, cubed

125ml water

¼ tsp salt

large pinch of cayenne pepper

freshly ground black pepper

70g plain flour

2 large eggs, lightly beaten with a fork

12 fresh chives, finely chopped (or 1–2 tsp finely chopped fresh thyme)

90g Cheddar cheese, grated

Preheat the oven to 220°C/200°C fan/gas mark 7. Line a baking sheet with non-stick baking paper or a silicone baking mat.

Place the butter, water, salt, cayenne and a few turns of freshly ground black pepper in a saucepan set on a low heat to melt the butter, then bring to the boil.

Sift the flour onto a piece of baking parchment. As soon as the butter and water mixture comes to the boil, pour the flour into the pot. Remove from the heat and stir vigorously until everything is well mixed. Reduce the heat to low, return the pot to the heat and cook for 2–3 minutes, stirring all the time, until the dough pulls away from the sides of the pot and begins to coat the base of the pot. Remove the pan from the heat and allow to rest for 2 minutes.

Beat the eggs a little at a time into the mix with a hand mixer. The batter may look like it has split, but don't worry – keep beating and it will come back together. Remember that you may not need all the egg. The batter should drop gently from a spatula with a gentle nudge.

Fold in the chives and about three-quarters of the grated cheese and stir until well mixed. Place the mixture into a pastry bag fitted with a wide plain tip and pipe the dough onto the prepared baking sheet in evenly spaced mounds, making each one about the size of a small cherry tomato.

Top each puff with a little of the remaining cheese, then transfer the baking sheet to the oven. Bake for 10 minutes, then turn the oven down to 190°C/170°C fan/gas mark 5 and bake for a further 20–25 minutes, until the puffs are completely golden-brown.

Remove from the oven, allow to cool slightly on a wire rack and serve warm. These can be made in advance and stored in an airtight container, then reheated in an oven set to 200°C/180°C fan/gas mark 6 for 3–4 minutes.

SERVES 8

CEVICHE OF SEA BASS WITH LIME & MANGO SALSA

As with sushi, make sure you get the freshest fish possible when making ceviche. Tell your fishmonger what you're making and he will give you the freshest fish. I usually call in a day or two ahead to give them notice, which they do appreciate. Also ask for the largest fillets you can get, as this makes it easier to prepare this dish. In the recipe I have removed the skin, as you do not eat this. However, depending on the thickness of the fillet this is not always possible, in which case you can cut this up with the skin on and allow your diners to remove this themselves.

INGREDIENTS

For the ceviche:

600g sea bass fillets

zest and juice of 3 limes

olive oil, for drizzling

salt and freshly ground black
  pepper

For the lime and mango
  salsa:

1 ripe mango

1 tbsp olive oil

½ tbsp soy sauce

1 tbsp honey

1 tbsp chopped fresh
  coriander leaves

½ tsp dried chilli flakes

Remove the skin from the fish fillets. Place the fillet on a chopping board skin side down. Holding the tail end firmly, with a sharp, flexible knife cut into the fish close to the tail of the fillet towards the skin and then slice towards the opposite end of the fish. Keep the knife as flat as you can to cut as close to the skin as possible along the full length of the fillet. Discard the skin.

With a sharp knife, remove the bloodline from down the length of the fish in the centre. This is a line of dark meat that runs the length of the fillet. This is achieved by cutting at an angle down into the fish on either side of the bloodline. Remove the dark meat and discard it.

Cut the fish into diamond shapes or thin strips.

Place the fish in one layer in a ceramic dish. Pour over the lime juice, cover in cling film and place in the fridge.

Cut the mango in half down the sides of the flat stone that runs through the centre of the fruit so that you end up with two fleshy halves. Take one half of the mango and make four parallel cuts through the flesh down to the skin. Make sure you don't cut through the skin. Turn the mango a quarter of a turn and cut four parallel cuts through the flesh down to the skin, but again not through the skin. Now push the mango from the skin side to turn it inside out and slice away the chunks of mango flesh that stand out of the skin. Repeat with the second half. Discard the skin and trim the flesh from around the stone. Cut the mango into small dice.

To make the salsa, mix all the ingredients in a bowl and leave to infuse, stirring occasionally.

When ready to serve, remove the fish from the fridge. Assemble on a plate. Sprinkle the lime zest over the fish, drizzle with a little olive oil and season lightly with salt and freshly ground pepper. Add the salsa to the plate.

Serve immediately.

MAKES
12

BRUSCHETTA WITH RICOTTA, PEAR & PROSCIUTTO

This is a twist on the traditional bruschetta. Make sure you cut the bread at a nice angle and not too thick.

INGREDIENTS

ciabatta bread

olive oil

100g smooth ricotta

1–2 tbsp honey

1 ripe firm pear

1 lemon, juiced

200g sliced prosciutto, torn into strips

basil leaves

freshly ground pepper

Preheat the oven to 200°C/180°C fan/gas mark 6.

Cut the ciabatta thinly at an angle into twelve slices. Brush olive oil lightly over both sides of the ciabatta slices. Arrange in a single layer on a baking tray and bake in the oven for 5–10 minutes, until lightly toasted, turning once. Allow to cool completely.

Meanwhile, mix together the ricotta and honey to taste.

Peel and core the pear, cut into small dice and place in a small bowl. Pour over the lemon juice to stop the pear from discolouring.

Spread a layer of the honey ricotta over the ciabatta slices. Place a teaspoon of diced pear on top. Twist the strips of prosciutto and place on top to add some height.

Garnish with torn basil, drizzle with a little olive oil and season with a turn of the pepper mill.

AVOCADO HUMMUS ON PASTRY CROUSTADE

Hummus is a great dip and the avocado not only adds to the flavour, but delivers an amazing colour too.

INGREDIENTS

1 x 400g tin of chickpeas, drained and rinsed

1 ripe avocado

1 large red onion, finely diced

1 red chilli, deseeded and finely chopped

1 garlic clove, finely grated

juice of 1–2 limes

sour cream, to serve

1 small bunch of fresh coriander, leaves only

For the croustade:

1 sheet of ready-rolled all-butter puff pastry

pinch of smoked paprika

Preheat the oven to 200°C/180°C fan/gas mark 6. Line a large baking tray with non-stick baking paper. I use flat baking trays, as you will need two of these that sit snugly together.

To make the croustade, lay the pastry on a board and stamp out discs with a 4cm pastry cutter. You should aim to get about thirty-six discs. Lightly dust the pastry discs with smoked paprika and transfer to the prepared baking tray. Lay a second sheet of non-stick baking paper on top of the pastry discs, then put another baking tray on top of this. The weight of the second tray will stop the puff pastry discs from rising as they bake.

Bake in the oven for 20–25 minutes. When removed from the oven, the pastry discs should be golden and crisp. Leave them to cool on a wire rack.

Place the chickpeas in a food processor and pulse until they appear chopped. Don't blitz them to a paste.

Cut the avocado around the middle lengthways, remove the stone and scrape the flesh into a large clean bowl. Mash to a coarse texture with a fork. Add the chickpeas, red onion, chilli, garlic and some of the lime juice. Mix well and taste. If you like it a bit sharper, you can add a little more lime juice.

To assemble, spread some avocado hummus over each pastry croustade. Add a dollop of sour cream and garnish with a fresh coriander leaf.

Stunning
Starters

WARM SALAD OF GAMBAS WITH STRAWBERRIES & STRAWBERRY VINAIGRETTE

You will often hear the term 'bringing a dish to the next level' on cookery programmes, which usually refers to heightening the flavours. In this dish, the strawberry flavour is heightened by the strawberry vinaigrette.

INGREDIENTS

6 tbsp rapeseed oil

salt and freshly ground black pepper

18 large gambas, peeled, deveined and patted dry with kitchen paper

vegetable oil

1 bag of mixed salad leaves

125g fresh strawberries, hulled and cut in half

For the strawberry vinegar:

250ml good-quality white wine vinegar

125g fresh strawberries, hulled and cut in half

To make the strawberry vinegar, pour the white wine vinegar into a glass jug and add the strawberries. Cover and leave to infuse for 48 hours in a cool place.

Transfer the vinegar and strawberries to a fine sieve over a clean bowl and allow to drain naturally – don't crush the strawberries, as this will cloud the vinegar. Pour the strawberry vinegar into a glass bottle with a tight seal and store in a cupboard away from direct sunlight for up to a month.

To make the vinaigrette, place the rapeseed oil and 3 tablespoons of the strawberry vinegar in a blender or spice grinder and blitz together to emulsify. Season with salt and pepper to taste.

To cook the gambas, place a pan on a high heat and brush the gambas on both sides with a little vegetable oil. When the pan is hot, add the gambas and fry for 4–5 minutes, turning regularly, until they turn pink and opaque. Remove from the heat and keep warm.

Place the salad leaves in a bowl and dress with the strawberry vinaigrette.

To serve, place a handful of dressed leaves on each plate. Arrange the gambas and strawberries on top and drizzle a little more strawberry vinaigrette around the salad.

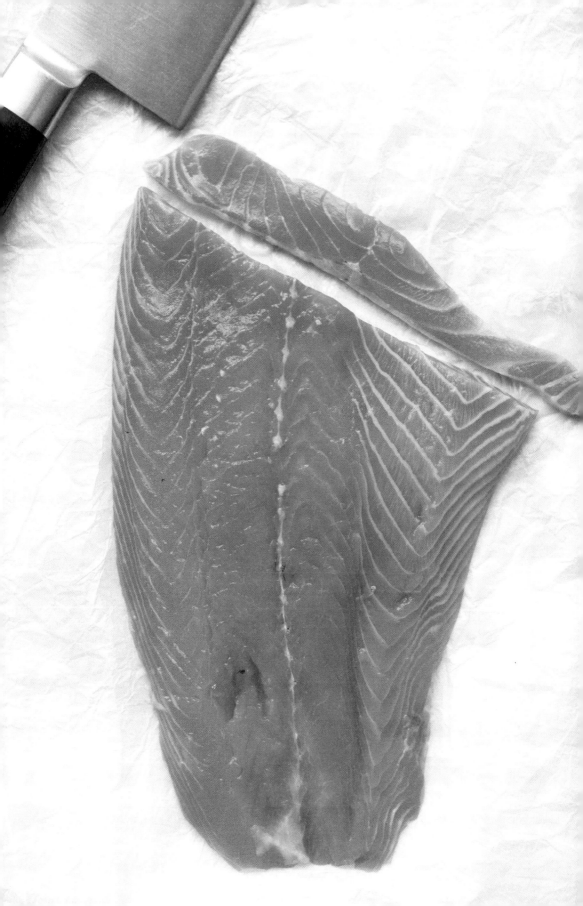

SALMON PARCELS WITH TOMATO COMPOTE

INGREDIENTS

salt and freshly ground black pepper

6 x 75g portions of salmon fillet, skin removed

olive oil

6 slices of white bread, crusts removed

25g butter

2 handfuls of rocket leaves

For the coriander pesto:

25g fresh coriander, with stalks

25g fresh flat-leaf parsley

1 spring onion, finely chopped

1 garlic clove, grated

50ml olive oil

1 tbsp pine nuts, toasted

1½ tsp freshly squeezed lemon juice

couple of pinches of cayenne pepper

For the tomato compote:

450g ripe tomatoes, peeled and finely chopped

1 tbsp vegetable oil

55g onion, finely sliced

1 small garlic clove, finely grated

1 x 400g tin of chopped tomatoes

splash of balsamic vinegar

1 tbsp chopped mixed fresh herbs, such as thyme, parsley and basil

This recipe is a little fiddly to prepare, but the texture of the crisp bread and the soft salmon is truly spectacular, making it well worth the effort. Take the time to make the parcels as neat as you can, as this will add to the wow factor of your finished dish.

Place everything required for the pesto in a food processor and blitz. Season with salt and chill until required.

To make the compote, first you need to peel the tomatoes. To do this, bring a pot of water to the boil, then reduce the heat to a simmer. Have a bowl of iced water on the side. Remove the core of each tomato by inserting a small knife into the tomato at a slight angle, just deep enough to remove the core, and cutting in a circle. Then cut a small X in the bottom of the tomato. Carefully place the tomatoes in the pot of simmering water. Once the skin begins to lift away from the X, remove the tomatoes with a slotted spoon and place in the bowl of iced water. Once the tomatoes are cool, the skin will peel off easily.

Place a pan on a medium heat. When the pan is hot, add the oil, then add the onion and garlic and sweat for about 10 minutes, until softened.

Add the tinned tomatoes, season and cook for about 10 minutes, until the tomatoes break down. Add the fresh chopped tomatoes and continue to cook until the compote has reduced to a sauce consistency.

Add a little balsamic vinegar and check the seasoning, then remove from the heat and add the mixed fresh herbs.

Meanwhile, season the salmon well and drizzle with a little olive oil.

If you have a pasta machine, roll the bread through it on the thinnest setting. Otherwise roll it as thin as possible with a rolling pin. Cut the bread into strips that are the same width as the salmon and big enough to encase the fish. Roll each fillet in a piece of bread, then trim the edges (this should look something like a spring roll only with the ends open). Chill until needed, seal side down (where the bread meets).

Preheat the oven to 200°C/180°C fan/gas mark 6.

Heat a frying pan over a medium heat and add the butter and a little oil. Once the butter begins to foam, add the salmon parcels, seal side down. Cook for 1–2 minutes, gently rolling the parcels to fry on all sides so that the bread will be golden all over. Transfer the parcels to a baking tray and place in the oven for 5–6 minutes, until cooked through.

Place the rocket in a bowl, toss with a generous amount of olive oil and season with a little salt.

To serve, place the rocket on the plates. Place a salmon parcel on top, then add a teaspoon of the pesto on the top of the parcel. Add a spoonful of the compote on the side.

BAKED COMTÉ TART WITH RED ONION MARMALADE

This is an amazing tart and the cheese and onion combination is particularly sublime. The secret to great pastry is to keep everything really cold. Make sure that you don't roll the pastry too thick, as this will cause a soggy bottom.

INGREDIENTS

For the pastry:

175g plain flour, plus extra for dusting

110g cold, salted butter, cut into small cubes, plus extra for greasing

2–3 tbsp cold water

For the red onion marmalade:

25g butter

2 red onions, finely sliced

50g soft dark brown sugar

4 tsp red wine vinegar

3 tsp water

freshly ground black pepper

For the filling:

4 free-range eggs

350ml double cream

150g Comté (or any hard cheese), grated

1½ tsp ground nutmeg, or to taste

1 tsp paprika, or to taste

salt and freshly ground black pepper

To make the pastry, combine the flour and cold butter in a food processor and add just enough cold water to bind the dough together. Wrap the pastry in cling film and chill for 30 minutes.

Preheat the oven to 200°C/180°C fan/gas mark 6.

To make the marmalade, melt the butter in a pot set over a medium heat, then add all the ingredients except the pepper. Cook for 15–20 minutes, stirring often, until the onions are soft and the marmalade has thickened. Season to taste with freshly ground black pepper.

To make the filling, beat the eggs lightly in a large bowl and stir in the cream. Stir in the cheese and season with the nutmeg, paprika, salt and pepper.

Lightly brush a 23cm fluted loose-bottomed tart tin with melted butter, dust with flour and shake out the excess. Roll the pastry out and use it to line the tin. Trim the edges neatly.

Carefully pour in the filling until it is almost to the top of the tin.

Bake in the oven for 15 minutes, then turn the heat down to 160°C/140°C fan/gas mark 3 for another 15 minutes. The filling should be set and the pastry should be golden.

Cut into wedges, allow to cool and serve with a crisp green salad and the red onion marmalade on the side.

SERVES
4

BEETROOT & ORANGE CAPPUCCINO

I use the term 'cappuccino' here to refer to the presentation of this starter. I serve these in glass cups so that you can see the amazing deep ruby purple of the beetroot against the stark white of the froth.

INGREDIENTS

450g small beetroots

olive oil

1 onion, finely diced

450ml chicken stock

zest and juice of 1 orange

salt and freshly ground
    pepper

50ml full-fat milk

Preheat the oven to 200°C/180°C fan/gas mark 6.

Brush the beetroots lightly with a little oil, then wrap them in tinfoil. Place them on a baking tray and roast for 30–40 minutes until cooked through. Remove from the oven, allow to cool slightly, then peel and roughly chop.

Place a pan on a medium heat, add 2 tablespoons of oil and when the oil is heated add the onion and sweat gently until soft and translucent.

Add the beetroot and the stock and bring to the boil. Reduce the heat and simmer for 5 minutes.

Remove from the heat, add half the orange zest and the orange juice and blend with a hand blender. Pass through a fine sieve and return to the pot. Season with salt and freshly ground pepper to taste and keep warm on a very low heat.

Place a small pan on a low heat, add the milk and whisk constantly. As the milk warms up a beautiful froth will form on the top.

Divide the soup between four serving glasses, spoon the froth on top to create the cappuccino effect and sprinkle with the reserved orange zest.

SERVES 6-8

SMOKED SALMON & SOUR CREAM TART WITH ROUGH PUFF PASTRY

If you're short on time it's okay to use shop-bought puff pastry, but please use a good-quality all-butter pastry for this recipe. It's a little more expensive, but the difference is vast.

INGREDIENTS

plain flour, for dusting

1 portion of homemade rough puff pastry (page 252) or shop-bought all-butter puff pastry

1 egg, beaten

1 medium onion, finely sliced

2 tsp olive oil

salt and freshly ground black pepper

250g sour cream or quark cheese

8 slices of Donnybrook Fair smoked Irish salmon

2 sprigs of fresh dill

juice of 1 lime

Preheat the oven to 200°C/180°C fan/gas mark 6.

Lightly dust your work surface with flour, then roll out the pastry to 14 x 9 inches. Place the pastry on a baking tray and brush the surface all over with the beaten egg. With a sharp knife score a line three-quarters of the way through the pastry all the way around about half an inch inside the edge of the pastry to create a border. Lightly prick the base inside the border with a fork.

Toss the sliced onion in the olive oil and season with some salt and pepper. Sprinkle the onions all over the base of the tart keeping inside the border line and bake in the oven for 15–20 minutes, until the pastry is crisp and golden. Remove from the oven and allow to cool completely.

Transfer the pastry to a cutting board. Spread the sour cream all over the base and then tear strips of salmon to place over the top. Garnish with fresh dill, tearing the small fronds apart, and drizzle with lime juice.

Cut into portions and serve with a simple salad.

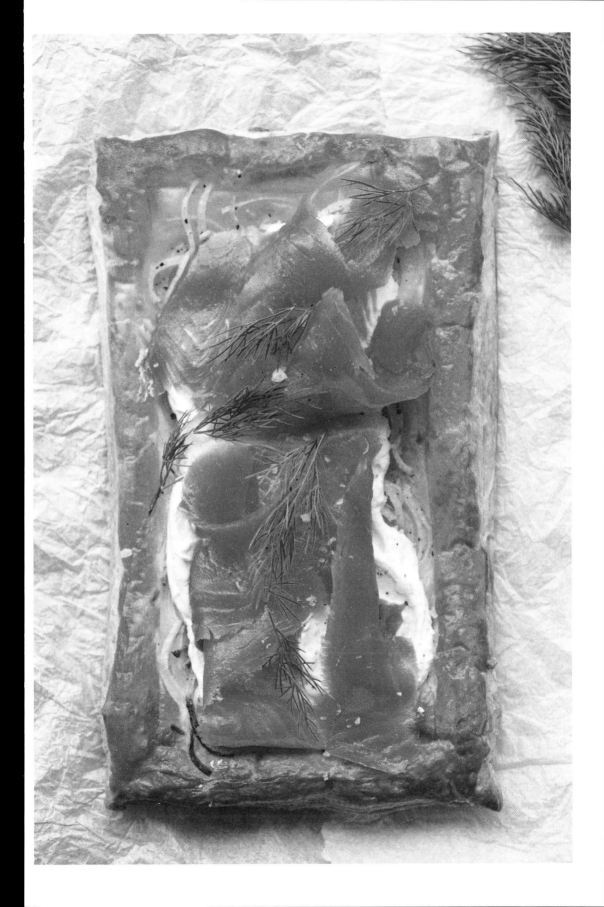

WARM SALAD OF ROAST PEARS WITH CARAMELISED RED ONIONS & GORGONZOLA DRESSING

INGREDIENTS

For the caramelised red onions:

olive oil

250g red onions, finely sliced

2 tbsp brown sugar

2 tbsp balsamic vinegar

sprig of thyme

sprig of rosemary

water

For the roast pears:

1 red chilli, sliced

1 stem lemongrass, chopped finely

1 cinnamon stick broken into pieces

½ tsp ground allspice

30ml cider vinegar

120g Demerara sugar

150ml water

4 ripe pears, cut in half and cored

For serving:

handful of whole almonds

150g Gorgonzola cheese

mixed salad leaves

I appreciate that there are two warm salads in this section but I absolutely love the surprise on friends' faces when they come around to dinner and are presented with this dish. Part of the appeal is that we rarely get to enjoy warm salads, so it is a pleasant surprise when one is offered.

Preheat the oven to 220°C/200°C fan/gas mark 7.

Place a pan on a medium heat, add some oil and when hot add the finely sliced onions. Cook until they begin to caramelise.

Add the sugar, balsamic vinegar and herbs and continue cooking until the onions are completely soft and the juice is syrupy. If you think the onions are drying out a little then add some water from time to time.

Leave to cool, then remove the herb stalks, strain off and reserve the excess liquid, and set aside.

Place the almonds on a baking tray and roast for 5–10 minutes. Watch them carefully so they do not burn. You will know they are ready when they release a beautiful almond aroma. Remove from the oven, cool and roughly chop.

Reduce the oven to 200°C/180°C fan/gas mark 6.

Mix together all the ingredients for the pears in a bowl, except the pears themselves.

Toss the pears in the mix, then place the pears and marinade in a small ovenproof dish.

Cook for approximately 1 hour or until the pears are cooked but holding their shape. Remove them from the oven and cool them to room temperature. Cut the pears into quarters.

Place the cheese and the strained juices from the onions into a small pan and melt the cheese a little over a low heat, mixing well to create the dressing.

Arrange the salad leaves, pears and some onions on a plate, drizzle over some of the dressing and scatter with the chopped almonds. Serve immediately.

Sensational
Salads

SERVES 4

WARM WINTER VEGETABLE SALAD

This salad is the perfect celebration of our great winter vegetables. Remember that we eat with our eyes, so take your time chopping the vegetables to make sure that they are all the same size and shape. I always include this recipe in the knife skills classes here at the cookery school, as it's a good test for the students. The evenness of the vegetables will dramatically improve the visual effect of the dish upon presentation.

INGREDIENTS

handful of walnut halves

2 parsnips

2 carrots

2 beetroots

1 celeriac

1 sweet potato

1 red onion

olive oil

salt and freshly ground black pepper

handful of crumbled feta

For the dressing:

1 bunch of fresh parsley, chopped

3 tbsp rapeseed oil

1 tbsp cider vinegar

½ tbsp balsamic vinegar

½ tbsp wholegrain mustard

½ tbsp honey

pepper

Preheat the oven to 200°C/180°C fan/gas mark 6.

Place the walnuts on a baking tray and roast in the oven for 5–10 minutes. Watch carefully so they don't burn. You will know they are ready when they release a beautiful walnut aroma. Remove from the oven and allow to cool, then roughly chop them.

Peel all the vegetables and remove the centre core from the parsnips. Cut the vegetables into even bite-sized pieces. Place all the chopped vegetables in a bowl, drizzle with olive oil and season with salt and pepper.

Place on a baking tray and roast for 30–40 minutes. The vegetables should be cooked but still have a little bite. Remove from the oven and allow to cool slightly.

Place all the ingredients for the dressing in a blender and blitz. Check the seasoning by tasting it and adjust with salt and pepper if required.

Toss the warm roasted vegetables in the dressing and place on a serving dish. Scatter the chopped toasted walnuts and crumbled feta on top.

SERVES
4

MOROCCAN ORANGE SALAD

This is a wonderfully fragrant salad. It is very important to remove the segments of orange from the membrane during the process of preparing this salad. This salad is very refreshing in its own right and also goes really well with Moroccan-inspired chicken or lamb dishes.

INGREDIENTS

20g flaked almonds

6 large oranges, peeled and segmented

4 Medjool dates, finely chopped

juice of ½ lemon

½ tsp ground cinnamon

1 tbsp icing sugar

2 tsp orange flower water

Place a dry pan on a low heat. Once heated, add the flaked almonds and toast them, stirring regularly. You only need the lightest of colour on these, so watch carefully as they can burn very easily.

Place the orange segments in a bowl with the chopped dates.

Add the lemon juice, cinnamon, icing sugar and orange flower water. Mix everything together. Leave aside to allow all the flavours to infuse.

When ready to serve, transfer the oranges to a serving dish and garnish with the flaked almonds.

COURGETTE & RED ONION LINGUINI WITH LEMON & CASHEW

Contrary to what you might think, this isn't a pasta dish. The linguini refers to the shape of the courgettes. Nut-based sauces are becoming a big food trend. Remember to soak the nuts, as the softer they are, the creamier and smoother the dressing will be.

INGREDIENTS

1 red onion, thinly sliced

small handful of raw cashews

3 courgettes

100g rocket leaves

For the dressing:

120g raw cashews

60ml rapeseed oil

120ml water

1 large garlic clove, grated

20g fresh mint

juice and grated zest of ½ lemon

pinch of sea salt

Place the raw cashews for the dressing in a bowl, cover with water and leave to soak for 2 hours to soften.

Place the thinly sliced red onion in a separate bowl, cover with water and leave to soak for 30 minutes.

Preheat the oven to 220°C/200°C fan/gas mark 7.

Place the handful of cashews on a baking tray and roast in the oven for 5–10 minutes, until they have taken on a little colour and you get a wonderful cashew aroma. Be careful, though, as these can burn really easily. Remove from the oven and allow to cool completely, then roughly chop.

Drain the other cashews and place in a blender with the rapeseed oil, water, garlic, mint and lemon zest and juice. Blend well. Taste the dressing and season with salt.

Using a julienne peeler (or just a regular vegetable peeler if you don't have a julienne peeler), peel long, thin strips from all sides of the courgettes, but only as far as the seeds in the centre. You can discard the seeds. Place these courgette strips in a large bowl.

Drain the red onion, pat dry with kitchen paper and add to the courgette. Add the rocket to the bowl and dress the salad with the cashew dressing.

Place on a serving dish and garnish with the chopped roasted cashews.

FETA, WATERMELON & CUCUMBER SALAD WITH ROASTED ALMONDS

Whenever I'm invited to a barbecue, this is the salad that I bring. I always enjoy bringing the Donnybrook Fair Cookery School to my friends' homes. The colour and flavour combinations of this salad are amazing and the crunch of the almonds adds a great texture to the salad. I tend not to dress the salad until I arrive, to keep it fresh.

INGREDIENTS

½ red onion, thinly sliced

handful of almonds

½ watermelon, cut into bite-sized pieces

1 cucumber, peeled, deseeded and cut into bite-sized pieces

handful of fresh mint leaves, finely sliced

100g feta cheese, crumbled

For the dressing:

60ml olive oil

20ml lemon juice

salt and freshly ground black pepper

Place the thinly sliced red onion in a bowl, cover with water and leave to soak for 30 minutes.

Preheat the oven to 220°C/200°C fan/gas mark 7.

Place the almonds on a baking tray and roast in the oven for 5–10 minutes, until they have taken on a little colour and you get a wonderful almond aroma. Be careful, though, as these can burn really easily. Remove from the oven and allow to cool completely, then roughly chop.

Drain the red onion and pat dry with kitchen paper. Dry the watermelon pieces too, to remove any excess moisture, and place in a large bowl with the red onion and cucumber.

To make the dressing, place the oil and lemon juice in a blender and blitz to emulsify. The dressing should be the consistency of a sauce. Season with salt and pepper to taste.

Add the fresh mint to the salad, then toss the salad in the dressing.

Place on a serving dish and garnish with the chopped roasted almonds and the crumbled feta.

ASIAN SALAD

As with most Asian food, this salad is all about presentation. It's also a good exercise for your knife skills, as you should try to make sure all the ingredients are cut to a similar length and size. This will add greatly to the overall presentation of the dish.

INGREDIENTS

1 cucumber, peeled, deseeded and sliced at an angle

1 carrot, coarsely grated into long strips

½ large red pepper, deseeded, membrane removed and thinly sliced

2 spring onions, thinly sliced at an angle

handful of dry-roasted peanuts

generous handful of fresh coriander leaves, chopped

For the dressing:

2 garlic cloves, grated

1 red chilli, deseeded and very finely diced

1 tbsp lime juice

1 tbsp soy sauce

½ tbsp fish sauce

1–2 tsp palm sugar or light brown sugar

1 tsp rice wine vinegar

Mix the cucumber, carrot, red pepper and spring onions in a large bowl.

In a separate bowl, whisk together all the ingredients for the dressing. Taste and adjust the flavour. If the dressing is too spicy, for example, you can add a little more sugar; if it's not spicy enough, you can add more fresh chilli.

Dress the salad and mix well. Scatter with the peanuts and freshly chopped coriander leaves and serve.

AUTUMN COLESLAW

The pomegranate seeds add a lovely textural aspect to this coleslaw and give fabulous bursts of flavour as you crunch through them.

INGREDIENTS

100g walnut halves

1 pomegranate

¼ red cabbage, cored

1 fennel bulb, outer layer removed

3 carrots, peeled

2 raw beetroots

sea salt and freshly ground black pepper

2 Granny Smith or Cox's apples

handful of fresh tarragon leaves, chopped

For the dressing:

2 organic free-range egg yolks

1 tbsp honey

1 tbsp good-quality mayonnaise

1 tbsp natural yogurt

1 tbsp cider vinegar

1½ tsp Dijon mustard

1 tsp pomegranate molasses

200ml mild rapeseed oil

Preheat the oven to 220°C/200°C fan/gas mark 7.

Place the walnuts on a baking tray and roast in the oven for 5–10 minutes. Watch carefully so they don't burn. You will know they are ready when they release a beautiful walnut aroma. Remove from the oven and allow to cool, then roughly chop them.

Cut the pomegranate in half and remove the seeds by gently tapping the skin side with a wooden spoon, allowing the seeds to fall into a bowl. Discard any of the bitter white membrane that may fall into the bowl.

In a food processor, finely shred the red cabbage and the fennel bulb and transfer to a large bowl, then finely grate the carrots and beetroots and add to the bowl too.

To make the dressing, put the egg yolks in a bowl. Add the honey, mayonnaise, yogurt, vinegar, mustard and pomegranate molasses and whisk. Once combined, season with some salt and pepper, then slowly pour in the rapeseed oil, whisking all the time to emulsify.

Leave the skin on the apples and grate them, discarding the core. Add to the bowl with the other vegetables and season with salt and pepper.

Add the dressing and toss gently to ensure an even coating on all the ingredients.

Place on a large serving dish and scatter with the chopped toasted walnuts, pomegranate seeds and chopped tarragon.

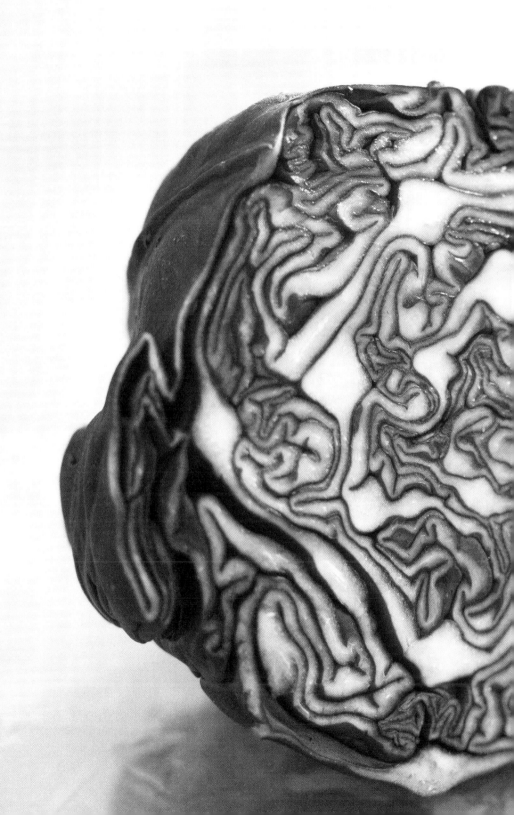

Winter &
Summer Soups

SMOKED HADDOCK CHOWDER

Every restaurant has its own version of chowder. Some include practically everything that swims in the sea, but this version is simplicity itself and places the flavour of the smoked haddock centre stage. We include this recipe in most of the classes we run for our visitors in the cookery school, particularly those from the United States.

INGREDIENTS

25g butter

225g leeks, finely sliced

100g onions, finely sliced

salt and freshly ground black pepper

3 medium potatoes, peeled and cut into small dice

400ml full-fat milk

400ml fish stock

200g smoked haddock, skinned and cut into small chunks

2 tbsp cream

2 tbsp chopped fresh flat-leaf parsley

Melt the butter in a pan set over a low heat, then sweat the leeks and onions with some salt and pepper for 4–5 minutes, until soft. Cooking on a low heat will ensure the leeks and onions don't take on any colour.

Add the potatoes, milk and stock to the pan. Bring to the boil, then reduce the heat and simmer for 5–10 minutes, until the potatoes are cooked.

Add the smoked haddock and cook for a further 2–3 minutes, until the fish is just cooked. Add the cream and season with salt and pepper, then stir in the chopped parsley. Serve in big, warmed bowls.

PEA & MINT SUMMER SOUP

This is a vibrant soup in both taste and colour. Don't put a lid on the pot at any stage of the cooking, as this dramatically reduces the green vibrancy of the soup. If you don't like things a little spicy, you can leave out the green chilli.

INGREDIENTS

1 tbsp olive oil

knob of butter

4 spring onions, sliced, plus a few extra to serve

1 small potato, peeled and cut into small dice

1 green chilli, deseeded and finely diced (optional)

500ml hot vegetable stock

225g frozen petit pois

small bunch of fresh mint, leaves picked, plus a few extra to garnish

salt and freshly ground black pepper

Heat the olive oil and butter in a heavy-based pan. When the butter is foaming, add the spring onions, potato and chilli, if using. Sweat gently over a medium heat without colouring for about 5 minutes.

Stir in the stock and bring to the boil. Reduce the heat and simmer for 10 minutes, until the potato is tender.

Stir in the peas and bring to the boil again, then cook for about 3 minutes, until they are just cooked through.

Remove the pan from the heat and allow to sit for 2–3 minutes, then add the mint leaves and whizz in a blender or food processor until smooth. Season with salt and pepper and serve with a few extra mint leaves on top.

SPANISH CHICKPEA & CHORIZO SOUP

This is the first soup recipe I teach to the children in the classes here at the cookery school in Donnybrook Fair. It is so simple and packed with amazing flavours that the kids love.

INGREDIENTS

1 tbsp olive oil

70g chorizo, diced

1 small onion, finely diced

1 celery stalk, finely diced

1 garlic clove, crushed or grated

400g tin chickpeas (unsalted)

400g tin chopped tomatoes (or 8 fresh ripe tomatoes, peeled and chopped)

500ml chicken stock

salt and pepper

large handful of spinach, destalked and finely chopped (or baby spinach leaves left whole)

Place the olive oil in a large saucepan on the heat and add the diced chorizo. Cook for 1–2 minutes until the chorizo releases its oils, then add the onion, celery and garlic. Cook on a gentle heat with the lid on for about 10 minutes until the onion is completely cooked. Then remove the lid, turn up the heat and cook for 1 minute to slightly brown the onion.

Add all the contents of the tin of chickpeas, the contents of the tin of tomatoes and the stock. Season with salt and pepper and bring to the boil. Simmer for about 20 minutes until the tomatoes are soft and the chickpeas have absorbed all the flavours. Taste for seasoning, add more salt and pepper if necessary. With the mixture still simmering add the spinach and cook for 1 minute more, until the spinach is soft.

Serve in big warm bowls.

FRESH CORN SOUP

One of the great joys of mastering the technique of making soup is that you can be really creative about the ingredients you add once you follow the basic process. Use fresh corn on the cob when it's in season, but you can substitute this with good-quality tinned sweetcorn at other times of the year.

INGREDIENTS

6 ears of corn (or 400g tinned sweetcorn)

25g butter

1 large onion, finely diced

1 medium potato, peeled and chopped into small dice

1.2 litres chicken stock

salt and freshly ground black pepper

fresh cream, to garnish

3 tbsp mixed chopped fresh herbs, such as thyme, basil, parsley and chives

Carefully cut down the length of the ears of corn to remove the kernels. Don't discard the cobs, as these are added to the soup to boost the flavour while cooking.

Place a large pan on a medium heat and melt the butter in it. Add the onion and sweat for 4–5 minutes, until soft and translucent.

Add the fresh corn kernels and the cobs, the diced potato and the stock and bring to the boil. If using tinned corn, don't add it at this stage. Instead, you should add the corn for the last 3–4 minutes of cooking.

Reduce to a simmer and cook for about 10 minutes, until the corn and potatoes are cooked through. Remove the cobs and discard. Season with salt and freshly ground black pepper.

Blend the soup with a hand-held blender but don't purée it, as you want to keep some texture in the soup. Check the seasoning and add more salt and pepper if required.

Serve drizzled with a swirl of cream and garnish with the chopped fresh herbs.

TOMATO CONSOMMÉ

This is not a consommé in the purest sense, but the result is as you would expect from a consommé with very little work. This can be served warm or cold. In summer I serve this with little balls of cucumber cut with a melon baller and frozen like ice cubes.

INGREDIENTS

14 large ripe tomatoes, roughly chopped

1 cucumber, peeled and roughly chopped

handful of mixed fresh herbs, such as chives, basil, chervil and dill

½ tbsp salt, plus extra for seasoning

freshly ground white pepper

For the garnish:

2 ripe tomatoes, peeled, seeds removed and flesh diced

1 cucumber, peeled, deseeded and diced

sprigs of fresh herbs, such as basil, chervil and dill

extra virgin olive oil, for drizzling

Place the chopped tomatoes and the cucumber in a bowl with the herbs and salt. Stir well, cover with cling film and allow the flavours to infuse at room temperature for a couple of hours.

Put the tomatoes, cucumber and herbs in a food processor fitted with the metal S-blade and pulse until the herbs are very finely chopped, but don't blitz to a purée.

Pour into a muslin-lined nylon sieve set over a large bowl. (Try not to use a metal sieve, as the acid in the tomatoes will react with the metal and impair the flavour slightly.) Cover with cling film and allow to drain overnight in the fridge. Do not press the contents through the muslin, as this will make the end result cloudy. (Afterwards, you can freeze the sieved pulp and add it to the next batch of tomato sauce that you make.)

Remove from the fridge and check the seasoning. Season with salt and freshly ground white pepper.

Meanwhile, to prepare the garnish, first you need to peel the tomatoes. To do this, bring a pot of water to the boil, then reduce the heat to a simmer. Have a bowl of iced water on the side. Remove the core of each tomato by inserting a small knife into the tomato at a slight angle, just deep enough to remove the core, and cutting in a circle. Then cut a small X in the bottom of the tomato. Carefully place the tomatoes in the pot of simmering water. Once the skin begins to lift away from the X, remove the tomatoes with a slotted spoon and place in the bowl of iced water. Once the tomatoes are cool, the skin will peel off easily and you can deseed and dice them.

To serve warm, gently heat the consommé in a pan, but be careful not to let it boil. Place some diced tomatoes and cucumber in a serving dish and pour over the warmed consommé. Scatter with some fresh herbs and a drizzle of olive oil.

To serve cold, place some diced tomatoes and cucumber in a serving dish and pour over the chilled consommé. Garnish as above and serve with three frozen cucumber balls in each bowl (see the introductory note).

SERVES
4

ASIAN BROTH

This recipe always reminds me of my time in Singapore. In restaurants there they would bring a large pot of this type of broth to the table. There was a heat source under the pot that kept the broth simmering and we would poach different ingredients in the broth: prawns, shredded pork or chicken, vegetables and noodles. I really enjoyed the atmosphere and the idea of cooking our own dinner in a restaurant. It's great fun recreating this experience in the cookery school here at Donnybrook Fair.

INGREDIENTS

1 head of pak choi

1 shallot, finely sliced

1 small chilli, deseeded and finely chopped

900ml chicken stock

juice of 1 lime

1½ tbsp tamari or soy sauce

1 tbsp honey

200g of your choice of pork or chicken fillet, finely sliced, or prawns, shelled and deveined

200g medium egg noodles

2 spring onions, thinly sliced, and fresh coriander, to garnish

Remove the leaves from the pak choi and set aside. Chop the rest of the pak choi into bite-sized pieces.

Place the shallot, chilli, chicken stock, lime juice, tamari and honey in a pot and bring the broth to a simmer. Check the flavour and adjust if necessary. If it's too sweet, add more tamari; too salty, add a little more honey. If you like it sharper, add more lime juice.

Now add your choice of meat, whether it's prawns, finely sliced pork or chicken. Also add the sliced pak choi (not the leaves) and noodles. Simmer the prawns for 3–5 minutes, or the finely sliced meat for 5–7 minutes, until cooked through. Make sure that the broth is on a very gentle simmer – if the broth is boiling, the prawns or meat will overcook and become tough. An instant-read food thermometer is very useful for ensuring that the meats are cooked (see the guide on internal temperatures on page 19).

Just before serving add the pak choi leaves to wilt in the broth. Then ladle into warmed bowls and garnish with the spring onions and coriander.

Cooking Meat
to Perfection

ASIAN FILLET OF PORK

I find that many people rarely cook pork as they have awful memories of dry meat. The secret to beautifully moist pork is to make sure that it's cooked to perfection. Serve the pork with the spiced plum sauce on page 237.

INGREDIENTS

1kg pork fillet, trimmed of all fat and silver tissue (approximately 2 large pork fillets)

olive oil

1 bag of mixed baby leaf salad

plum sauce (page 237), to serve

For the marinade:

2 garlic cloves, grated

1 x 5cm piece of fresh ginger, peeled and grated

2 tbsp tamari or soy sauce

2 tbsp hoisin sauce

2 tbsp treacle

1 tbsp olive oil, plus extra for brushing

1 tbsp sesame oil

1 tsp Chinese five spice

Place all the marinade ingredients in a small bowl and mix well. Pour into a large ziplock plastic bag. Add the pork fillet to the bag and shake well. Seal the bag and place it in the fridge for 6–8 hours, or overnight if possible, as it improves the flavour. Turn the bag over every couple of hours.

Remove the pork fillet from the marinade and pat dry with kitchen paper, then brush lightly with some olive oil. Allow to rest at room temperature for 1 hour.

Heat a barbecue to a medium heat, then cook the pork for 20–30 minutes, turning regularly, until the thickest part of the fillet has reached a temperature of 75°C on an instant-read food thermometer. If you don't have a food thermometer, insert a skewer into the meat and make sure the juices run clear.

Alternatively, preheat the oven to 200°C/180°C fan/gas mark 6. Place an ovenproof frying pan on a high heat. When the pan is smoking hot, sear the pork quickly on all sides. Transfer the pan to the oven and roast for 20–30 minutes, until the thickest part of the fillet has reached a temperature of 75°C on an instant-read food thermometer. If you don't have a food thermometer, insert a skewer into the meat and make sure the juices run clear.

Arrange the salad leaves on a platter, slice the pork and arrange it on top of or beside the salad leaves. Warm the plum sauce and pour it over the pork, then serve straight away.

CARAMELISED FILLET OF BEEF

In the cookery school I find it much easier to teach students how to cook a fillet of beef correctly in one piece as opposed to individual steaks. Once the beef is cooked and rested, you can slice it to the thickness required. Serving the beautifully caramelised beef with caramelised onions (page 212), potato wedges (page 221) and mushroom sauce (page 238) is a fabulous comfort dinner.

INGREDIENTS

200g treacle or blackstrap molasses

100ml water

800g fillet of beef (even thickness along the length), trimmed

2 garlic cloves, skins left on and smashed

freshly ground black pepper

3–4 tbsp groundnut or vegetable oil

Mix the treacle with the water, then pour into a ziplock bag. Add the beef and garlic and rub to coat the beef. Place in the fridge to marinate for 24 hours.

Remove the beef from the bag and pat it dry with kitchen paper, then season with freshly ground black pepper. Set aside at room temperature for 1 hour.

Meanwhile, place the marinade in a pot and reduce to a sticky glaze.

Preheat the oven to 220°C/200°C fan/gas mark 7.

Lightly brush the beef with groundnut or vegetable oil. Place an ovenproof pan on a high heat until the pan is smoking hot, then quickly sear the beef on all sides. Transfer to the oven and roast until the beef is cooked to your liking. Test the meat by sticking an instant-read food thermometer into the centre of the thickest part of the fillet and make sure it has reached the desired temperature (see the chart on page 19). If you don't have a food probe, then roast for about 20 minutes for rare, 30 minutes for medium and 40 minutes for well done.

Remove from the oven and brush with the glaze. Allow to rest on a wooden board, loosely covered in tinfoil, for 15–20 minutes before carving.

SERVES 6

SPATCHCOCK CHICKEN

While you need to do a bit of surgery here, this is a great way to cook a chicken and is quicker than roasting one whole. Once you have mastered the process, you can marinate the chicken in any combination of flavours that you prefer. I have given some examples here to get you started. Always make sure that the chicken is removed from the fridge 1 hour before roasting.

INGREDIENTS

1 x 1.5kg free-range chicken

25g butter, melted

salt and freshly ground black pepper

Remove the chicken from the fridge 1 hour before you plan to roast it and allow it to come to room temperature.

Preheat the oven to 200°C/180°C fan/gas mark 6.

Place the chicken on a board, breast side down and with the legs pointing towards you. Using a sharp knife or poultry shears, cut along both sides of the backbone the full length of the bird and remove the backbone. Turn the chicken over, open the bird out and press down hard between the two fillets to flatten the bird.

Now insert two skewers diagonally through the breast and thighs of the bird forming an X shape. These will keep the chicken flat when cooking.

With a sharp knife, cut two parallel slashes through the meat down to the bone in each of the legs. This allows the heat to penetrate the chicken legs.

Pat the chicken skin with kitchen paper to remove any moisture on the skin. Brush the chicken all over with the melted butter and season with salt and pepper.

Place on a roasting tray and roast in the oven for 40–45 minutes, until the chicken is cooked through. Check that the chicken is cooked by inserting your instant-read food thermometer into the centre of the breast and leg meat. It should be 75°C. If you don't have a food thermometer, insert a skewer into the meat and make sure any juices run clear.

Remove the chicken from the oven and place on a wooden board. Cover loosely with tinfoil and a tea towel and leave to rest for 20–25 minutes before carving.

MARINADES FOR THE CHICKEN

To get the maximum flavour from a marinade, you must marinate the chicken for at least 1 hour, but it's best if you leave it for a couple of hours or ideally overnight.

THAI RED CURRY:

INGREDIENTS

2 tbsp homemade (page 232) or shop-bought sweet chilli sauce

1 tbsp homemade (page 154) or good-quality shop-bought Thai red curry paste

zest and juice of 1 orange

1 garlic clove, grated

Place the sweet chilli sauce, red curry paste, orange zest and garlic in a bowl and mix together. Add the orange juice to loosen the paste.

Brush the paste over the chicken and leave in the fridge for a minimum of 30 minutes to marinate. Pour any remaining marinade over the chicken before roasting in the oven.

LEMON & THYME:

INGREDIENTS

2 tbsp olive oil

1 tsp chopped fresh thyme leaves

zest and juice of 1 lemon

2 garlic cloves, grated

Place all the ingredients in a bowl and mix well.

Brush over the chicken and leave in the fridge for a minimum of 30 minutes to marinate.

CHINESE FIVE SPICE:

INGREDIENTS

3 garlic cloves, grated

2 tbsp finely chopped fresh ginger

2 tbsp honey

2 tbsp light soy sauce

1 tbsp olive oil

1 tbsp rice wine

2 tsp Chinese five spice

Place all the ingredients in a bowl and mix well.

Brush over the chicken and leave in the fridge for a minimum of 30 minutes to marinate. The longer you leave it to marinate, the better the flavour will be.

SERVES
6

PAN-ROASTED CANNON OF LAMB

One of the great joys of the Donnybrook Fair Cookery School is its location and our proximity to the amazing butchers we have downstairs in the store. The cannon of lamb is from the eye of loin section. It's a beautifully tender piece of lamb and is treated exactly like cooking a fillet of beef. Ask your butcher to prepare this for you; you may need to order this the day before. The mint sauce on page 233 is perfect with this.

INGREDIENTS

3 x 500g cannon of lamb

1 tbsp rapeseed oil

freshly ground black pepper

2 sprigs of fresh rosemary

salt

Remove the lamb from the fridge 1 hour before you plan to start cooking and let it come up to room temperature.

Preheat the oven to 200°C/180°C fan/gas mark 6.

Brush the lamb lightly with the oil and season with freshly ground black pepper.

Heat an ovenproof frying pan over a medium heat. When it's smoking hot, sear the lamb quickly on all sides.

Place the rosemary under the lamb, then transfer it to the oven to roast for 4–5 minutes for rare, 5–8 minutes for medium, or 10–12 minutes for well done (see the chart on page 19).

Remove the lamb from the oven, season with salt and place on a wooden board. Cover loosely with tinfoil and set aside to rest for 5–10 minutes before carving into slices to serve.

STEAMED & BAKED HAM

Steaming is a great way to cook a ham. With this recipe, however, you need to go a step further. Once the ham is cooked, it's then baked. This leaves the ham beautifully moist and so easy to carve. If you're cooking this for Christmas, add some Christmas spices to the wine and stock, such as cinnamon sticks, star anise, cardamom pods or even an orange cut in half.

INGREDIENTS

1 x 1.5kg ham fillet

2 onions, peeled and cut in half

2 carrots, roughly chopped

1 head of garlic, cut in half

500ml chicken stock

½ bottle white wine

6 peppercorns

For the glaze:

2 tbsp wholegrain mustard

2 tbsp treacle

Place the ham in the top section of a steamer. Place all the other ingredients in the bottom section.

Cover the top with baking parchment and a piece of tinfoil that's slightly bigger than the steamer and place the lid firmly on top of the tinfoil. The tinfoil helps to seal the lid on tightly so that the steam doesn't escape.

Place the steamer on a high heat and bring to the boil, then reduce the heat to a simmer. Steam for approximately 1½ hours, until the internal core temperature is 75°C. Keep an eye on the wine and stock and make sure that it doesn't all evaporate. If it's running low, top up with water.

When it's cooked, remove the ham from the steamer, peel off the rind and set aside to cool completely.

Preheat the oven to 180°C/160°C fan/gas mark 4. Line a baking tray with non-stick baking paper.

To make the glaze, mix the mustard and treacle together in a small bowl. Place the ham on the lined tray and brush half of the glaze all over the ham.

Bake the ham in the oven for 20 minutes, then remove from the oven and brush the remaining glaze over the ham (also brush on any glaze that has gathered on the tray). Return to the oven and bake for another 20 minutes, then remove and brush with any glaze that has pooled on the tray.

Return to the oven for a further 10 minutes, then remove from the oven and allow to rest for 15 minutes before carving.

SERVES
6

ROAST DUCK

I have had plenty of opportunities to experiment with many different techniques for roasting duck over the years. A critical part of the process is in the preparation of the duck, so plan well ahead to ensure the best results.

INGREDIENTS

1 whole duck

1 small onion

1 orange

1 garlic bulb

Early in the day, remove the duck from the fridge and remove any excess fat from the cavity area. Place the duck on a wire rack on a draining board and pour a kettle of boiling water over the duck. Pat the duck dry and return it to the fridge, uncovered, for at least 2 hours to air dry.

Remove the duck from the fridge and allow it to come to room temperature. This should take roughly 1 hour.

Preheat the oven to 150°C/130°C fan/gas mark 2 as the duck comes to room temperature.

Prick the skin all over with a fork. Be careful to only puncture the skin and not the meat.

Cut the onion, orange and garlic in half and stuff them into the duck's cavity. Place the duck breast side down on a wire rack set in a roasting tray.

Roast in the oven for 1½ hours, then remove the duck from the oven, turn it breast side up and return to the oven for another 1½ hours. Check the tray and drain off any excess fat (this is great fat for roast potatoes, so don't discard it).

After the 3 hours are up, increase the oven temperature to 210°C/190°C fan/gas mark 7 and roast for a further 20–30 minutes, until the skin is golden and crispy.

Remove the duck from the oven and place on a wooden board. Don't cover it, though, as this will cause the skin to lose its crispiness. Leave to rest for 20 minutes before carving.

One-Pot
Wonders

CHICKEN, SQUASH & BABY POTATO CASSEROLE

This is a great introduction to casseroles as it's so easy to prepare. It's important to watch it carefully and reduce the heat to a simmer immediately after the boiling point is reached, as boiling the chicken will make it tough.

INGREDIENTS

2 tbsp olive oil

4 chicken legs, skinless

4 chicken thighs, skinless

2 garlic cloves, grated

2 tsp ground coriander

2 sprigs of fresh thyme, leaves picked

800ml chicken stock

½ butternut squash, peeled and cut into cubes

10–12 baby potatoes

200g French beans

50g black pitted olives

salt and freshly ground black pepper

Preheat the oven to 200°C/180°C fan/gas mark 6.

Heat the oil in a casserole dish, then add the chicken pieces and fry for 2–3 minutes, until golden. Don't crowd the pan, as this will cause the chicken to steam and not caramelise.

Add the garlic, coriander, thyme and stock. Bring to the boil, then reduce to a simmer and add the squash and potatoes. Cover with a lid and cook in the oven for 20–30 minutes, until the chicken is cooked through.

Lift out the chicken pieces and vegetables and set them aside in a warmed serving dish. Cover with tinfoil to keep them warm.

Boil the cooking liquid on the hob until it has reduced by half. Add the French beans and olives and simmer for 5–10 minutes, until cooked.

Season to taste, then pour the liquid over the chicken and vegetables to serve.

SWEET POTATO, SPINACH & LENTIL DAHL

Lentils are so nutritious, yet we rarely eat them. This dish is a celebration of red lentils with a combination of mild spices.

INGREDIENTS

2 tomatoes, peeled and chopped

100g dried red lentils

1 onion, finely chopped

1 red chilli, deseeded and finely chopped

450ml vegetable stock

1 tsp garam masala

½ tsp ground turmeric

1 large sweet potato, peeled and chopped into bite-sized pieces

2 handfuls of baby leaf spinach, shredded

natural yogurt, to serve

fresh coriander leaves, to garnish

First you need to peel the tomatoes. To do this, bring a pot of water to the boil, then reduce the heat to a simmer. Have a bowl of iced water on the side. Remove the core of each tomato by inserting a small knife into the tomato at a slight angle, just deep enough to remove the core, and cutting in a circle. Then cut a small X in the bottom of the tomato. Carefully place the tomatoes in the pot of simmering water. Once the skin begins to lift away from the X, remove the tomatoes with a slotted spoon and place in the bowl of iced water. Once the tomatoes are cool, the skin will peel off easily and you can chop them.

Put the lentils, tomatoes, onion, chilli, vegetable stock and spices in a pan. Simmer for 10–15 minutes, until the lentils are almost cooked (there should still be a little bite).

Add the potato and gently simmer until tender, which should take another 10–12 minutes.

Add the shredded spinach leaves into the dhal and cook, stirring, until wilted.

Serve with a spoonful of natural yogurt and garnish with fresh coriander leaves on top.

CHICKEN PILAF

This is a wonderfully fragrant dish. The secret with this dish is to ensure that when the lid goes on the pot the pilaf barely simmers. It is a fine balance of heat and timing, because if the pilaf boils the liquid will evaporate before the rice is cooked, but if the heat is too low then the rice will overcook.

INGREDIENTS

2 tbsp coconut oil

600g skinless, boneless chicken thighs or fillets, cut into bite-sized pieces

1 onion, finely diced

1 red chilli, deseeded and finely chopped

1 tbsp grated fresh ginger

1 tsp salt

1 tsp garam masala

¼ tsp ground cinnamon

½ tsp ground cloves

4 curry leaves

300g basmati rice

1 chicken stock cube dissolved in enough boiling water to make 700ml

230g frozen peas

80g flaked almonds

chopped fresh coriander, to garnish

chopped fresh mint, to garnish

Heat the coconut oil in a large pot with a snug lid on a medium heat. Add the chicken and fry for 2–3 minutes, until golden. You will need to do this in two batches so as not to crowd the pot and cause the chicken to boil. When cooked, move the chicken to a plate and keep warm by covering it with tinfoil.

Add the onion, chilli, ginger and salt to the pan and cook for 5 minutes. Add the spices and curry leaves and cook for a further minute to release the flavours. Add the rice and stir to coat, then return the chicken and all the juices on the plate to the pan.

Add the stock and increase the heat to high to bring to the boil, then reduce the heat to a bare simmer. Cover and cook for 12 minutes, until the stock has been absorbed and the rice is tender. Lift the lid after 2–3 minutes to make sure it's just gently simmering, then cover with the lid again for the remainder of the cooking time.

Remove from the heat and stir in the peas, then put the lid back on and leave to sit for 10 minutes.

Meanwhile, to toast the flaked almonds, place a pan on a low heat and add the almonds, stirring every 15–20 seconds until they begin to take on a very light colour. Remove from the heat and transfer to a plate to cool.

Add the toasted almonds and fluff up the pilaf with a fork. Transfer to a serving bowl and garnish with the chopped fresh herbs.

SERVES
4

MEDITERRANEAN SEAFOOD STEW

The sauce for this dish freezes really well, so you can make large batches and freeze it. Take out a portion before you go to work to defrost so that when you get home you only have to reheat it and add the seafood and herbs. Just be careful not to boil the seafood, as it will overcook and turn tough.

INGREDIENTS

4 ripe tomatoes, peeled and chopped

3 tbsp olive oil

1 onion, finely sliced

1 head of fennel, finely sliced

3 garlic cloves, grated

150ml white wine

1 x 400g tin of chopped tomatoes

500ml fish stock

pinch of caster sugar (optional)

salt and freshly ground black pepper

600g selection of firm white fish (such as cod, hake, monkfish) and seafood (prawns and scallops)

chopped fresh flat-leaf parsley, to garnish

First you need to peel the tomatoes. To do this, bring a pot of water to the boil, then reduce the heat to a simmer. Have a bowl of iced water on the side. Remove the core of each tomato by inserting a small knife into the tomato at a slight angle, just deep enough to remove the core, and cutting in a circle. Then cut a small X in the bottom of the tomato. Carefully place the tomatoes in the pot of simmering water. Once the skin begins to lift away from the X, remove the tomatoes with a slotted spoon and place in the bowl of iced water. Once the tomatoes are cool, the skin will peel off easily and you can chop them.

Place a pot on a medium heat and add the oil. When the oil is hot, add the onion, fennel and garlic. Reduce the heat and cook for about 5 minutes, until soft but not coloured.

Add the wine and leave to simmer until the wine has reduced to half its original volume. Add the tinned and fresh chopped tomatoes and the fish stock and cook for 30 minutes, then taste the sauce. Tinned tomatoes can be a little acidic, so if that's the case, then add a little sugar and taste again. Be careful, however, as even half a teaspoon can make a big difference. Season with salt and pepper to taste.

Add the fish and seafood and place the lid on the pot. Gently simmer for 4–5 minutes, until the fish, prawns and scallops are all cooked through.

Garnish with the chopped fresh parsley and serve straight away.

SERVES 4

MUSHROOM RISOTTO

I made this dish for the Italian ambassador during a private demonstration here in the cookery school, showcasing organic Italian produce. I'm pleased to say that he loved it. This recipe does take a bit of time, but the results are really worth the effort. It's very important to make sure that the stock is kept hot when it's added to the rice and you must also remember to gently stir throughout the process.

INGREDIENTS

3 tbsp extra virgin olive oil

225g chestnut mushrooms, sliced

1 onion, finely chopped

2 garlic cloves, grated

1½ litres vegetable stock

1 tbsp dried cep (porcini) mushrooms

100ml white wine

350g Arborio or Carnaroli rice

50g Parmesan, freshly grated, plus extra to serve

25g butter

salt and freshly ground black pepper

chopped fresh flat-leaf parsley, to garnish

Heat the olive oil in a saucepan set on a high heat. Add the chestnut mushrooms and fry for 4–5 minutes, until just cooked and golden. Transfer the mushrooms to a bowl and set aside.

Reduce the heat to medium and add the onions and garlic to the pot. Cook for 4–5 minutes, until the onions are soft but not coloured.

Place the stock in a separate medium-sized pot. Add the ceps to the stock and bring to a simmer. It's important that the stock is kept hot throughout the cooking process.

Pour the wine into the pot with the onions and garlic and reduce to roughly one-third its original volume. Add the rice and stir well. Reduce the heat to low so that the pot is just barely simmering.

Now start adding the hot stock a ladle at a time (leaving the ceps in the stock pot), stirring until all the liquid is absorbed. Don't add the next ladle of stock until the previous one has been almost completely absorbed by the rice. This process should take 15–20 minutes and you should be gently stirring the rice all the time.

Return the chestnut mushrooms to the rice and cook for 1–2 minutes to heat them through. Remove the pan from the heat and stir in the grated Parmesan and the butter.

Remove the ceps from the stock pot, finely chop them and stir them through the risotto.

Leave to rest for a few minutes, then season with salt and pepper and serve in warm bowls with some extra Parmesan shavings scattered on top and garnished with chopped parsley.

SERVES
4-6

DONNYBROOK FAIR JUMBO SAUSAGE & BEAN CASSOULET

I have used our own brand of jumbo sausages for this recipe (there are a variety of flavours, so pick whichever one you prefer), but this also works really well with Toulouse sausage.

INGREDIENTS

8 Donnybrook Fair jumbo sausages

2 tbsp olive oil

4 ripe tomatoes, peeled and finely chopped

2 onions, finely diced

2 carrots, finely diced

3 celery stalks, finely diced

2 large garlic cloves, grated

300ml white wine

1 x 400g tin of chopped tomatoes

bouquet garni (fresh parsley, thyme and bay leaf tied together with string)

150ml water

salt and freshly ground black pepper

1 x 400g tin of haricot beans, drained and rinsed

fresh flat-leaf parsley, chopped, to garnish

Preheat the oven to 200°C/180°C fan/gas mark 6.

Place a large casserole over a high heat. Brush the sausages lightly with 1 tablespoon of the oil and add to the heated casserole. Sear the sausages, turning regularly to brown them. Remove from the casserole and set aside on a plate and cover with tinfoil to keep warm.

Meanwhile, you need to peel the tomatoes. To do this, bring a pot of water to the boil, then reduce the heat to a simmer. Have a bowl of iced water on the side. Remove the core of each tomato by inserting a small knife into the tomato at a slight angle, just deep enough to remove the core, and cutting in a circle. Then cut a small X in the bottom of the tomato. Carefully place the tomatoes in the pot of simmering water. Once the skin begins to lift away from the X, remove the tomatoes with a slotted spoon and place in the bowl of iced water. Once the tomatoes are cool, the skin will peel off easily and you can finely chop them.

Add the remaining tablespoon of oil to the casserole and lower the heat to medium. Add the onions, carrots, celery and garlic. Sweat for 5 minutes, until soft, stirring all the time. Don't allow them to colour.

Add the wine and scrape the bottom of the casserole to release all the caramelised bits. Increase the heat and reduce the wine to half its initial volume.

Add the tinned and fresh tomatoes, the bouquet garni and the water. Stir well and season with salt and pepper. Add the beans and the sausages and cover with the lid, then cook in the oven for 45 minutes.

Remove the casserole from the oven. Remove the bouquet garni and leave to rest for 15 minutes before serving. Garnish with some chopped fresh flat-leaf parsley.

Curry Nights

CHICKEN KORMA

Before many students at the cookery school begin their training they shy away from making curries, as they consider them to be very hot. Once they come to the school, however, they learn how to control and balance the heat. Korma is a great introduction to curry, as it's such a mild dish. If you prefer it a bit hotter, you can just increase the amount of chilli pepper. It's important not to boil the sauce when you add the chicken, as this will cause the chicken to become tough.

INGREDIENTS

2 tbsp coconut oil

1 large onion, diced

3 garlic cloves, grated

4cm piece of fresh ginger, peeled and grated

4 whole cloves

4 cardamom pods, crushed

1½ tsp ground cumin

1 tsp mild chilli powder

½ tsp ground turmeric

¼ tsp ground allspice

1 tsp ground coriander

4 chicken fillets, cut into bite-sized pieces

100g ground almonds

450ml chicken stock

2 tsp tomato purée

250ml double cream

salt and freshly ground black pepper

75g flaked almonds

chopped fresh coriander, to garnish

basmati rice (page 155), to serve

Heat the oil in a large saucepan or frying pan set over a medium heat and fry the onion, garlic, ginger, cloves and cardamom pods for a few minutes, until the onion begins to soften. Add the remaining spices and stir them around the pan, allowing them to release their flavour.

Add the chicken and coat well with the spice mix. Add the ground almonds, chicken stock and tomato purée and bring to a simmer. Gently simmer for 30 minutes but don't allow to boil, as this will cause the chicken to become tough.

Add the cream and simmer until the sauce has reduced to the consistency of thick cream. Taste and adjust the seasoning.

Place the flaked almonds on a dry pan set over a medium heat and toast, turning regularly, until the nuts take on a light colour. Transfer to a plate to cool.

Scatter the chopped fresh coriander leaves over the curry along with the toasted almonds. Serve with basmati rice.

THAI RED PRAWN & BUTTERNUT SQUASH CURRY

This recipe also works well with chicken, so if you like, you can substitute chicken in place of the prawns. A wet and dry spice grinder is important here for the sauce, as it makes it really smooth. Shrimp paste can be purchased from most food halls or at any of the Asian markets.

When buying coconut milk it's important to get the brand with the highest coconut extract percentage. Some have a very low content and are combined with emulsifiers, which will disintegrate during cooking and cause your sauce to split. In the school we use coconut milk that is made from 96% coconut extract.

INGREDIENTS

1 tbsp coconut oil

1 small butternut squash, peeled, deseeded and cut into bite-sized pieces

250ml chicken stock

1 x 400g tin coconut milk (reserving 3 tbsp for the curry paste)

16 large prawns, shelled and deveined

4 spring onions, thinly sliced at an angle

chopped fresh coriander, to garnish

basmati rice, to serve (see opposite)

For the Thai red curry paste:

4 garlic cloves, chopped

1–2 red chillies, deseeded and chopped

1 shallot, chopped

1 stalk of fresh lemongrass, minced

1 thumb-sized piece of fresh galangal or ginger, peeled and sliced

3 tbsp thick coconut milk (or just enough to keep the blades turning)

2 tbsp freshly squeezed lime juice

2 tbsp fish sauce

2 tbsp soy sauce

2 tbsp tomato ketchup or good-tasting tomato purée

½ tbsp chilli powder (add more if you like it spicy)

1 tsp shrimp paste

1 tsp ground cumin

1 tsp caster sugar

¾ tsp ground coriander

¼ tsp ground white pepper

Place all the ingredients for the curry paste in a food processor or spice grinder and process well to create a smooth, fragrant Thai red curry paste. If it's too thick, add a little more coconut milk to help blend the ingredients.

Place a large pan on a high heat. Add the coconut oil and fry the paste in the oil for 1 minute, until fragrant. Add the butternut squash, stirring to coat evenly in the paste.

Add the stock and the remaining milk from the tin of coconut milk to create the curry sauce. Gently simmer for 5–7 minutes, until the squash is almost cooked through. Add the prawns and continue to gently simmer for another 3–5 minutes, until the prawns are cooked.

Garnish the curry with the spring onions and chopped fresh coriander. Serve with basmati rice.

SERVES
4

BASMATI RICE

This is the easiest way I know to cook perfect rice every time. You can use the same process for all rice, including jasmine and long-grain rice, although you should bear in mind that wild rice will take longer to cook.

INGREDIENTS

pinch of salt

400g basmati (or other) rice

4 tsp coconut oil (1 tsp per person)

Preheat the oven to 160°C/140°C fan/gas mark 3.

Place a large ovenproof pot of salted water on a high heat and bring to the boil. Add the rice and cook for 8–10 minutes, until it's al dente – it should be soft on the outside but still have a bite in the middle.

Drain the rice and return it to the pot. Gently stir through the coconut oil, cover the pot with a layer of tinfoil and press the lid firmly down to tightly seal the pot. Transfer to the oven for 15 minutes to continue cooking through steaming. The rice can be left in the oven for up to 45 minutes.

Remove from the oven and fluff up with a fork prior to serving.

MAKES
24

VIETNAMESE PORK BALLS

These little pork morsels are packed with flavour. These are usually served as a starter or as Asian tapas. They can be served wrapped in a Baby Gem lettuce leaf or on a cocktail stick with the dipping sauce on the side.

INGREDIENTS

2 shallots, chopped

2 sticks of lemongrass, outer leaves removed and core finely chopped

2 garlic cloves, grated

handful of fresh coriander

1 dessertspoon grated fresh ginger

3 tsp soy sauce

2 tsp fish sauce

1 tsp palm sugar

freshly ground black pepper

500g minced pork

coconut oil, for frying

Baby Gem lettuce leaves, to serve

For the dipping sauce:

1 garlic clove, chopped and very finely grated

4 tbsp freshly squeezed lime juice

1 tbsp palm sugar

1 tbsp fish sauce

1 tbsp water

fresh coriander leaves, to garnish

Put the shallots, lemongrass, garlic, coriander, ginger, sauces, sugar and pepper to taste into a food processor and blitz until they look to be chopped very finely.

Place the pork in a bowl, add the chopped ingredients and mix well.

Shape this mixture into twenty-four small balls.

Cover the balls with cling film and rest them in the fridge for 30 minutes.

For the sauce, combine everything except the coriander in a saucepan and heat gently. Stir to dissolve the sugar. Allow to cool and put into a serving bowl. Float a few coriander leaves on top.

Remove the pork balls from the fridge.

Place a pan on a medium heat and add 2 tablespoons of coconut oil.

Gently fry the pork balls for about 10 minutes, turning now and again until cooked through.

Serve them wrapped in a leaf of baby gem lettuce with the dipping sauce drizzled over.

SERVES 6-8

ONION BHAJIS

INGREDIENTS

vegetable oil, for deep fat frying

4 medium onions, thinly sliced

200g plain flour

300ml water

2 tbsp garam masala

1 tbsp cumin seeds

1 tbsp salt

1 tbsp tomato ketchup

1 tsp chilli powder

mint and cucumber raita (see below), to serve

Onion bhajis are a great addition to any Asian-inspired meal. They are really simple to make, but it's essential that the onion is finely sliced and the oil is clean and heated to the correct temperature. These can be cooked in a pan of oil heated to 180°C, but I am slow to recommend this method of frying as it can be dangerous.

Heat the oil in a deep fat fryer to 180°C.

Place all the ingredients in a bowl and mix well (the easiest way to do this is by hand).

When the oil is hot, gently drop a tablespoon of batter into the fryer. Fry for 3–4 minutes, turning occasionally in the oil to ensure the bhaji is cooked through. Transfer to a plate lined with kitchen paper to remove any excess oil and repeat with the remaining batter.

Serve the bhajis with a bowl of mint and cucumber raita on the side.

SERVES 6-8

MINT & CUCUMBER RAITA

INGREDIENTS

½ cucumber, peeled and deseeded

250ml natural yogurt

½–1 mild green chilli, deseeded and finely chopped

large handful of fresh mint leaves, chopped

large pinch of salt

Raitas are designed to cool spicy food. This is really versatile and can be served with onion bhajis (above) or samosas (page 162). Be sure you use a set yogurt or else the raita will be too loose.

Grate the cucumber into a clean tea towel, then squeeze out as much moisture as you can by wrapping it tightly in the towel.

Transfer to a bowl with all the other ingredients and mix well. Chill until required.

MAKES 12

PEA & POTATO SAMOSAS

This will bring out the amateur engineer in you as you fold the perfect sharp corners. This takes time and practice, so don't worry if the first few attempts aren't perfect. Keep going and you will master the technique.

INGREDIENTS

150g filo pastry

melted butter, cooled, for sealing the samosas

mint and cucumber raita (page 159) or sweet chilli sauce (page 232), to serve

For the filling:

150g potatoes

150g carrots

2 tbsp coconut oil

¼ tsp cumin seeds

1 medium onion, chopped

1 green chilli, deseeded and finely chopped

¼ tsp ground coriander

¼ tsp salt

pinch of garam masala

100g frozen peas, thawed

handful of fresh coriander leaves, chopped

To make the filling, peel and dice the potatoes and carrots to the size of a pea.

Place a pan of salted cold water on a high heat. Bring to the boil, then add the potatoes and carrots and cook for 2–3 minutes. Remove them from the boiling water and refresh in iced water. Once completely cooled (it will take about 1 minute), remove them from the iced water and place on kitchen paper to dry.

Heat the coconut oil in a pan set on a high heat. Add the cumin seeds and fry until they start to splutter, then reduce the heat to medium and add the onion and chilli. Fry for 6–7 minutes, until softened.

Mix in the coriander, salt and garam masala and stir-fry for 1 minute. Add the potatoes, carrots and peas and fry for a couple of minutes. Remove from the heat and allow to cool completely. This is very important, as otherwise the hot filling will melt the pastry. Stir in the chopped fresh coriander.

Preheat the oven to 180°C/160°C fan/gas mark 4. Line a baking tray with non-stick baking paper.

Unwrap the filo pastry and place it beside you on a clean work surface. Lay a clean tea towel over the pastry, as it will dry out very quickly if it's left uncovered.

Take one sheet of filo pastry and lay it on a board in front of you. Cut the filo pastry width-wise into three equal strips. Place a spoonful of filling at the top right corner of the pastry strip, just in from the edge. Don't be tempted to overfill, as this will make it difficult to fold.

Brush the edges of the pastry lightly with melted butter. Taking the top left-hand corner, bring the pastry over the filling and press along the edge where the pastry joins. Press the pastry down as close to the filling as possible.

Now take the top right corner and fold it directly towards you and place it on the right-hand edge. Keep folding the triangles over, right down to the bottom. Brush the last edge with a little more butter and seal. Repeat until all the filling is used up.

Place the samosas on the lined baking tray, brush the tops with melted butter and put in the centre of the oven. Bake for 25–30 minutes, turning them once halfway through cooking, until lightly browned and crisp.

Serve on a platter with a bowl of mint and cucumber raita or sweet chilli sauce on the side.

Tapas

FIELD & WILD MUSHROOMS WITH CRISPY BREAD

One of the most popular classes here at the cookery school is 'Tapas and the Wines of Spain'. I co-host the class with our head of wine, pairing different wines with each dish. It's a great way to learn about the relationship between food and wine.

This first tapas dish is a real celebration of mushrooms. You can use whatever combination of mushrooms that you prefer. Just don't cut the mushrooms thinly, as you want to keep the texture as they cook – if they're too thin, they will disintegrate. Brush the mushrooms to clean them instead of washing them, as they absorb water.

INGREDIENTS

1 loaf of ciabatta bread

2 tbsp olive oil, plus extra for brushing

500g mixed mushrooms (button, chestnut, shiitake), stalks removed and caps thickly sliced

1 garlic clove, grated

25g butter

sprig of fresh thyme, leaves picked

100ml cream

salt and freshly ground black pepper

2 tbsp chopped fresh flat-leaf parsley

Preheat the oven to 200°C/180°C fan/gas mark 6.

For the bread crisps, cut twelve thin slices of ciabatta at an angle. Brush lightly with oil and place on a baking tray. Bake in the oven for about 10 minutes, turning once, until lightly coloured and crisp. Remove from the oven and leave to cool on a wire rack.

Heat the 2 tablespoons of olive oil in a frying pan set over a medium heat. When it's hot, fry the mushrooms for about 3–4 minutes, until they begin to soften and take on some colour. Add the garlic and continue to fry for 30 seconds. Add the butter and thyme leaves and cook until the butter has melted, then add the cream and allow it to reduce and thicken. Remove from the heat and season with salt and pepper.

Place the crispy breads on a serving platter. Add a spoonful of the mushroom mix on top of each one and garnish with chopped fresh parsley. Serve warm.

SERVES 6

CHORIZO GLAZED WITH SHERRY & HONEY

This is a quick dish to prepare. Be careful with the heat, however, as the chorizo can burn easily.

INGREDIENTS

250g semi-cured whole chorizo

sunflower oil

2 garlic cloves, grated

4 tbsp sherry

1 tbsp runny honey

Peel the chorizo and slice it at an angle.

Heat a splash of oil in a pan set on a medium heat, then add the garlic and cook for 1 minute, stirring all the time to flavour the oil. Increase the heat to medium–high and add the chorizo. Fry for 3–4 minutes, until golden and crisp. Remove from the heat and drain off most of the fat.

Return the pan to the heat and add the sherry to deglaze the pan. Add the honey and reduce until the sherry and honey have formed a sticky sauce.

Transfer the chorizo and the sauce from the pan into a serving dish.

MAKES 1L

SANGRIA

This is a fantastic centrepiece to a tapas night. It is best to be organised and to start this the day before to allow all the flavours to infuse.

INGREDIENTS

750ml good-quality dry red wine

500ml lemonade

1 lemon

1 lime

1 orange

250g caster sugar

250ml white rum

250ml orange juice

Fresh mint leaves

Place the red wine and lemonade in the fridge overnight.

Cut the fruit in half lengthways and then cut thin slices across each half.

Place the fruit in a non-metallic bowl. Add the sugar and rum and stir well. Once stirred, cover the bowl with cling wrap and leave overnight.

Before your guests arrive transfer the fruit, rum and sugar into a large jug, add the wine and then dilute to taste with the lemonade and orange juice.

Add plenty of ice and torn mint leaves.

TORTILLA TAPAS

This tapas is baked in the oven in a cake tin. The secret here is to make sure that the tin is really hot before you add the mix so that a crust forms immediately, which means it will easily come out of the tin.

INGREDIENTS

3 tbsp olive oil, plus extra for brushing

3 medium potatoes, peeled and thinly sliced, stored in cold water

1 large onion, thinly sliced

1 large red pepper, quartered, deseeded and thinly sliced

2 garlic cloves, crushed

salt and freshly ground black pepper

6 large eggs, lightly beaten

handful of fresh flat-leaf parsley, chopped

½ tsp dried chilli flakes

Heat the olive oil in a pan set over a medium heat. Remove the potatoes from the water and dry them really well. Add the potatoes and onion to the pan and fry gently for 15 minutes, stirring frequently, until the potatoes are tender. Add the pepper and garlic and cook for 5 minutes more. Tip into a large bowl, season and allow to cool.

Preheat the oven to 200°C/180°C fan/gas mark 6.

When the potatoes and onion are cool, stir in the beaten eggs, parsley and chilli flakes. Leave to sit for 5 minutes, then put a non-stick fixed-bottom 20cm square tin in the oven to heat up. After 10 minutes, remove the tin and brush it lightly with oil. Pour in the egg mixture and return to the oven.

Bake in the oven for 15–20 minutes. Check if it's ready by pressing the top lightly. If it's still runny, return it to the oven for a couple more minutes. Once cooked, remove and leave to cool in the tin for 5 minutes, then turn out onto a board. Cut into sixteen squares and serve.

CREAMED SMOKED TROUT WITH CRISPY BREAD

This is such a simple dish to prepare and it also works really well with smoked mackerel.

INGREDIENTS

1 loaf of ciabatta bread

olive oil

3–4 smoked trout fillets, skin removed

200g Greek-style natural yogurt

1–2 tbsp prepared horseradish from a jar

2 tbsp freshly squeezed lemon juice

salt and freshly ground black pepper

chopped fresh flat-leaf parsley, to garnish

Preheat the oven to 200°C/180°C fan/gas mark 6.

For the bread crisps, cut twelve thin slices of ciabatta at an angle. Brush lightly with oil and place on a baking tray. Bake in the oven for about 10 minutes, turning once, until lightly coloured and crisp. Remove from the oven and leave to cool on a wire rack.

Flake the smoked trout into small pieces, removing any bones. Place in a food processor and pulse briefly. Add the yogurt, horseradish and lemon juice and pulse to the texture you like. Season with salt and freshly ground pepper.

Place the crispy breads on a serving dish and spoon the trout on top, then garnish with some chopped fresh parsley.

PAN-FRIED PRAWNS WITH MOJO VERDE

I recommend that you buy the gambas in their shells for this dish, as the quality is far superior. You need to do a little surgery to remove the heads, shells and digestive tracts, but it's a job worth doing. Alternatively, you can ask your fishmonger to do this for you.

INGREDIENTS

1 garlic clove, grated

2 tbsp olive oil

pinch of paprika

salt and freshly ground black pepper

12 gambas, shelled and deveined

For the mojo verde:

1 garlic clove, grated

small handful of fresh coriander, leaves only

small handful of fresh flat-leaf parsley, leaves only

1 small green pepper, deseeded and cut into bite-sized pieces

100ml olive oil

2 tbsp red wine vinegar

Place the garlic, olive oil, paprika and some salt and pepper in a bowl and mix to combine, then toss in the gambas and chill until required.

Place a pan on a high heat and, when the pan is hot, add the prawns and all the contents from the bowl. Fry the prawns, stirring regularly for 2–3 minutes until the prawns are cooked through.

To make the mojo verde, place the garlic, coriander and parsley in a food processor and blitz together. Add the pepper, oil and vinegar and blitz again. Season to taste and chill until required.

Serve the gambas on a platter with a bowl of the mojo verde on the side.

SPANISH ALBONDIGAS

INGREDIENTS

50g fresh white breadcrumbs

2 tbsp full-fat milk

4 Medjool dates, stoned and
finely chopped

4 spring onions, finely
chopped

2 garlic cloves, finely grated

1 red chilli, deseeded and
finely chopped

3 tbsp finely chopped fresh
flat-leaf parsley leaves

250g minced beef

250g minced lamb

1 medium egg, lightly whisked

½ tsp fine sea salt

½ tsp freshly ground pepper

3 tbsp olive oil

chopped fresh flat-leaf parsley,
to garnish

For the sauce:

2 large ripe tomatoes, peeled
and finely chopped

2 tbsp olive oil

1 small onion, finely diced

2 garlic cloves, grated

200ml good-quality sherry

1 x 400g tin of chopped
tomatoes

1 bay leaf

salt and freshly ground black
pepper

½ tsp caster sugar (optional)

Meatballs are an absolute must when hosting a tapas night. This recipe is highly adaptable, so you can mix any combination of minced meats: beef, lamb, chicken, pork or even turkey. The addition of the breadcrumbs soaked in milk makes sure that the meatballs are light and moist.

Place the breadcrumbs in a large bowl and pour over the milk. Leave to rest at room temperature while you prepare the rest of the ingredients for the meatballs.

Add the dates, spring onions, garlic, chilli and parsley to the breadcrumbs and mix well, then add the minced meats, egg, salt and pepper. Mix well, but be careful not to over mix, as this will make the meatballs tough.

Dampen your hands with some cold water and roll the mix into twenty-four even-sized balls. Place on a baking tray and chill in the fridge for 30 minutes while you prepare the ingredients for the sauce.

To peel the tomatoes for the sauce, bring a pot of water to the boil, then reduce the heat to a simmer. Have a bowl of iced water on the side. Remove the core of each tomato by inserting a small knife into the tomato at a slight angle, just deep enough to remove the core, and cutting in a circle. Then cut a small X in the bottom of the tomato. Carefully place the tomatoes in the pot of simmering water. Once the skin begins to lift away from the X, remove the tomatoes with a slotted spoon and place in the bowl of iced water. Once the tomatoes are cool, the skin will peel off easily and you can finely chop them.

Remove the meatballs from the fridge and place a large frying pan on a medium heat. When the pan is hot, add the 3 tablespoons of olive oil. Gently fry the meatballs for 4–5 minutes, until golden-brown all over. You will need to do this in batches so as not to crowd the pan. Remove from the pan and place on a clean tray. Cover with tinfoil to keep warm while you make the sauce.

To make the sauce, return the pan to a medium heat and add 2 tablespoons of olive oil. When the oil is hot, add the onions and garlic and gently cook for 4–5 minutes, until the onions have softened.

Increase the heat to high and add the sherry. Allow the sherry to bubble away until it has reduced to about one-third of its original volume.

Add the chopped fresh tomatoes along with the tinned tomatoes and the juice from the tin. Add the bay leaf and reduce the heat to a gentle simmer. Allow the sauce to simmer for 10–15 minutes, until thickened.

Season the sauce with salt and pepper and taste. If it's a little sharp, stir in the sugar.

Add the meatballs to the sauce and gently simmer for 10–12 minutes, until the meatballs are cooked through. If you have an instant-read food thermometer, the core temperature should be 75°C.

Remove the pan from the heat and transfer the sauce and meatballs to a serving dish. Garnish with some freshly chopped parsley and serve hot.

Easy
Seafood

SERVES 4

PAN-STEAMED COD WITH CHORIZO

Many students at the cookery school are wary of cooking fish at first. Steaming is a really easy and foolproof way to cook fish and therefore overcome that initial hesitation. Once the potatoes and chorizo are cooked, the fish is laid on top of them. Then you simply place the lid on the pan and steam them to perfection.

INGREDIENTS

1 tbsp extra virgin olive oil, plus extra to serve

75g semi-cured whole chorizo, peeled and thinly sliced

200g baby Rooster potatoes, sliced and placed in cold water to stop them going brown

salt and freshly ground black pepper

100ml dry sherry

large handful of cherry tomatoes, halved

4 thick cod fillets, skin removed

30g fresh flat-leaf parsley, chopped

crusty bread, to serve

Heat a large frying pan (one that has a lid) on a medium heat, then add the oil. When the oil is hot, add the chorizo. Fry for 2 minutes, until it starts to release its oils. Dry the potatoes well and add them to the pan. Stir to coat the potatoes with the oil and season with salt and pepper.

Add half of the sherry and cover the pan tightly. Leave to cook for 10–15 minutes, until the potatoes are just tender. Keep an eye on the potatoes, stirring them every so often.

When the potatoes are half cooked through, add the tomatoes and place the lid back on the pan.

When the potatoes are almost completely cooked through, season the fish well, then place the fillets on top of the potatoes, chorizo and tomatoes.

Add the remaining sherry, put the lid on again and leave to cook for 5 minutes, until the fish has turned white and is flaky when prodded in the middle.

Scatter the whole dish with the parsley and drizzle with a little extra virgin olive oil. Serve straight away with the crusty bread.

BEER-STEAMED MUSSELS WITH FRITES

These mussels are served with frites, aka skinny fries (see page 225). La Chouffe is a light, fragrant beer that won't overpower the mussels and is available from any of the Donnybrook Fair stores. (If you can't source Le Chouffe, then Duvel will work brilliantly as well.)

INGREDIENTS

1kg fresh mussels

20g butter

2 shallots, finely diced

1 garlic clove, grated

150ml La Chouffe beer

100ml double cream

30g fresh flat-leaf parsley, chopped

salt and freshly ground black pepper

frites (page 225), to serve

Wash the mussels under cold running water. Scrape off the barnacles and pull off any beards. If any are open, tap them gently on the table to close them. Discard any that don't close.

Place a heavy-based pot with a tight-fitting lid on a medium heat. Melt the butter, then add the shallots and garlic and cook for 1 minute.

Add the beer and increase the heat, then add the mussels and place the lid on the pot. Steam the mussels for 3–4 minutes, shaking the pot every so often.

Remove the pan from the heat and check that all the mussels are open. Discard any that are still closed. Remove them from the pot with a slotted spoon and cover with tinfoil to keep warm.

Return the pot to the heat, add the cream and bring to a simmer. Remove from the heat and add the freshly chopped parsley. Taste and adjust the seasoning if required.

Divide the mussels between four serving bowls and pour over the sauce. Serve with the frites on the side.

SERVES
4

LOIN OF MONKFISH WRAPPED IN SERRANO HAM

This is a beautifully simple way to cook monkfish. Ask your fishmonger to trim the fish (remove the thin membrane under the skin), as this can be a difficult job if you aren't used to doing it.

INGREDIENTS

4 x 200g monkfish loins, well trimmed

12 wafer-thin slices of Serrano ham

vegetable oil, for brushing

Earlier in the day, remove the fish from the fridge. Depending on the size of the slices of Serrano ham, lay out two or three slices to create a wrap that will fit around each monkfish loin, covering its entire length. Wrap each monkfish loin in a single layer of Serrano ham, then wrap each one tightly in cling film. Return to the fridge for a couple of hours before cooking. This will help the monkfish to hold its shape.

If you have any Serrano ham left over, preheat the oven to 190°C/170°C fan/gas mark 5. Place the extra slices on a baking tray and roast for 5–6 minutes, until crispy. Set aside to serve with the fish.

Preheat the oven to 220°C/200°C fan/gas mark 7.

Remove the fish from the fridge, take off the cling film and lightly brush the outer layer of Serrano ham with a little vegetable oil.

Place a heavy-based, ovenproof non-stick pan on a high heat. When it's hot, quickly sear the fish all over, turning it regularly to ensure an even golden colour. Transfer the pan to the oven and roast for 7–8 minutes, until the fish is cooked through.

PAN-FRIED MACKEREL WITH HORSERADISH CREAM

The secret to this dish is to achieve a really crispy skin on the fish. Skin that isn't crispy is unpalatable. To do this, the skin must be really dry, so place the mackerel on a plate, skin side down, dry well with kitchen paper and return to the fridge for at least 1 hour to allow the skin to dry completely.

INGREDIENTS

100g crème fraîche

1–2 tbsp good-quality prepared horseradish from a jar

1 tbsp chopped parsley

1 tbsp vegetable oil

4 mackerel fillets

salt

Mix the crème fraîche with 1 tablespoon of horse-radish in a small bowl, then taste it. If you prefer a slightly stronger flavour, add the second tablespoon of horseradish, then add the parsley.

Place a heavy-bottomed, non-stick pan on a high heat. When it's hot, add the oil and allow it to heat up.

Season both sides of the mackerel fillets lightly with salt. Add the fillets to the pan skin side down, as this will be the presentation side. Gently press the fillets down to make sure that they don't curl up and to make sure that all of the skin stays in direct contact with the pan.

Fry the fish for 3–4 minutes, then gently turn over. The skin should be golden and crispy. Fry for a further minute, until cooked through. Remove the mackerel from the pan and place on a serving plate, skin side up.

To serve, add spoonfuls of the horseradish cream on the side.

SALMON, FETA &
CUCUMBER TART

Cucumber and salmon is a well-established combination of flavours. This is a really easy tart to assemble and looks fabulous when brought to the table.

INGREDIENTS

½ unwaxed lemon

300g salmon fillet, pin-boned and skin removed

1 bunch of fresh dill

4 spring onions, finely chopped

1 small cucumber, peeled, deseeded and chopped into bite-sized pieces

100g feta cheese, crumbled

2 eggs, lightly beaten

salt and freshly ground black pepper

3 sheets of filo pastry

rapeseed oil

Zest the lemon, then cut it in half and place it in a large pot, reserving the zest for later. Add the salmon fillets and some of the fresh dill to the pot and cover everything with cold water.

Place the pan on a high heat and bring to the boil, then reduce to a simmer. Simmer for about 15 minutes, until the salmon is cooked through. Remove from the heat and allow the salmon to cool down completely in the poaching liquid.

Preheat the oven to 180°C/160°C fan/gas mark 4.

When it's completely cold, remove the salmon from the liquid and flake the fish into a large bowl. Add the spring onions, cucumber, feta, eggs, 2 tablespoons of chopped fresh dill and the lemon zest. Mix well and season with salt and pepper.

Carefully unroll the three sheets of filo pastry and cut them in half. Take half a sheet of pastry and brush it lightly with some rapeseed oil. Drape it to one side of a 22cm loose-bottomed tart tin, oil side down, so that some of the pastry hangs over the side. Make sure the overhang is enough to reach the centre of the tart tin when folded in to the centre. Brush another piece of pastry with oil and place in the tin, overlapping slightly with the first piece. Repeat with the rest of the pastry – the aim is to have the sheets covering the base of the tin with enough excess hanging over the edge to fold back over to completely cover the tart. Pour the filling into the tart tin and spread into an even layer. Fold the pastry overhang into the middle and scrunch it up, making sure the filling is covered. Brush with a little more oil.

Bake the tart in the oven for 30 minutes, until the pastry is crisp and golden-brown. Remove the tart from the oven and allow it to cool slightly before carefully removing it from the tin.

Slice into wedges and serve.

SERVES
4

HERB-CRUSTED HAKE FILLETS

This recipe makes a regular appearance in our fish class at the cookery school. It's a great introduction to cooking fish well, as roasting is one of the easiest ways to cook fish to perfection.

INGREDIENTS

25g butter

4 slices of day-old wholemeal bread, crusts removed

3 tbsp chopped fresh mixed herbs, such as parsley and chives

zest of 1 unwaxed lemon

pinch of grated fresh nutmeg

salt and freshly ground black pepper

4 thick hake fillets, pin-boned and skin removed

1 small egg yolk, beaten

Preheat the oven 200°C/180°C fan/gas mark 6. Line a baking tray with non-stick baking paper.

Melt the butter in a small pan and leave to cool.

Blitz the bread in a food processor to fine crumbs. Tip into a bowl and stir in the cooled butter, herbs, lemon zest and nutmeg and mix well. Season with salt and pepper.

Brush the hake fillets lightly with a little beaten egg yolk. Top each fillet with a quarter of the crumb mix and press down lightly. Transfer to the lined baking tray.

Bake in the oven for 15–20 minutes, until the hake is cooked through and the crumbs are crisp and golden.

Sushi

SUSHI SEASONING

You can buy good-quality sushi seasoning at Asian markets, but you can also make your own at home. Sushi should be served with pickled ginger (readily available from most super-markets), wasabi and sushi soy sauce.

INGREDIENTS

3½ tsp Japanese rice vinegar

1½ tsp caster sugar

1 tsp salt

1 piece of kombu

Place all the ingredients in a plastic or ceramic bowl. Whisk firmly to make sure everything is well mixed.

Store in a sealed container for up to six months. Mix 45ml of seasoning (removing the kombu) to every 200g of cooked rice.

NIGIRI

Nigiri are small oval shapes of rice with a wide variety of ingredients neatly pressed on top.

INGREDIENTS

8 tbsp cooked sushi rice (page 205)

8 small dots of wasabi

8 thin slices of very fresh salmon, tuna, poached chicken or mango

Using one damp hand, mould a tablespoon of rice into an oval-shaped ball. Place a small dot of wasabi on top. Place a slice of very fresh salmon, tuna, poached chicken or mango on top and shape into an oval around the top of the rice.

Repeat seven times. Serve straight away.

SWEET CHILLI CHICKEN MAKI

Make sure you have all the ingredients prepared before you start, as you will need to work quickly and efficiently.

INGREDIENTS

1 chicken breast

2 tbsp sweet chilli sauce (page 232)

2 sheets of nori

400g cooked sushi rice (page 205)

8 rocket leaves

pickled ginger, to serve

wasabi, to serve

soy sauce, to serve

Place the chicken breast in a small pan and cover completely with water. Place on a high heat and bring to the boil, then reduce the heat to a gentle simmer and cook for 12–15 minutes, until the chicken is cooked through. Remove from the heat and allow to cool, then shred the chicken and mix with the sweet chilli sauce.

Place one sheet of nori on a sushi rolling mat, shiny side down and with the long side facing towards you. Using wet hands, spread an even layer of cooked sushi rice on the nori, leaving a 2cm sliver of nori visible at the side farthest away from you. Don't squash the rice or make the layer too thick – you should be able to see the nori through the rice.

Spoon half of the chicken in a line across the nori about halfway up the rice, then place half of the rocket on top of the line of chicken.

To roll the sushi, fold the mat over, starting at the side closest to you and tucking in the end of the nori to start the roll. Keep rolling, lifting up the mat as you go and keeping the pressure even but gentle until you have finished the roll.

You don't need to moisten the top edge of the nori with water to seal the sushi roll closed. If you leave the roll with the join underneath, the moisture in the roll will seal the edge for you. If any filling falls out the sides, just push it back in. The edges may look ragged, but don't worry.

Remove the roll from the mat and place on a board to dry out before cutting. The roll will firm up after 10 minutes; if you try to cut it any sooner, it will be too soft.

Repeat with the remaining ingredients.

Cut each roll into eight even-sized pieces with a wet, very sharp knife. If you don't use a sharp knife, the roll will be squashed as you cut it.

Arrange the pieces on a plate. Serve with pickled ginger, wasabi and soy sauce.

MAKES
1 ROLL / 8
PORTIONS

SPICY TUNA MAKI

When buying your tuna, make sure you tell your fishmonger that it's for sushi and he will make sure you get the freshest possible tuna. Shichimi powder is a mix of several spices that can be sourced from any good Asian store.

INGREDIENTS

150g very fresh tuna, finely chopped

4 spring onions, finely chopped

1 tsp soy sauce, plus extra to serve

pinch of shichimi powder

1 sheet of nori

200g cooked sushi rice (page 205)

pickled ginger, to serve

wasabi, to serve

Mix the chopped fresh tuna with the spring onions, soy sauce and a pinch of shichimi powder in a small ceramic bowl.

Place a sheet of nori on a sushi rolling mat, shiny side down and with the long side facing towards you. Using wet hands, spread an even layer of cooked sushi rice on the nori, leaving a 2cm sliver of nori visible at the end farthest away from you. Don't squash the rice or make the layer too thick – you should be able to see the nori through the rice.

Spoon the tuna in a line across the nori about halfway up the rice.

To roll the sushi, fold the mat over, starting at the side closest you and tucking in the end of the nori to start the roll. Keep rolling, lifting up the mat as you go and keeping the pressure even but gentle until you have finished the roll.

You don't need to moisten the top edge of the nori with water to seal the sushi roll closed. If you leave the roll with the join underneath, the moisture in the roll will seal the edge for you. If any filling falls out the sides, just push it back in. The edges may look ragged, but don't worry.

Remove the roll from the mat and place on a board to dry out before cutting. The roll will firm up after 10 minutes; if you try to cut it any sooner, it will be too soft. Cut it into eight even-sized pieces with a wet, very sharp knife. If you don't use a sharp knife, the roll will be squashed as you cut it.

Arrange the pieces on a plate. Serve with pickled ginger, wasabi and soy sauce.

MAKES
1 ROLL / 8
PORTIONS

ISO CALIFORNIA ROLL

A California roll is best described as an inside-out sushi roll, since the rice is on the outside. This is more technical, as you will be flipping the roll over to fill it, but laying the nori on cling film will make the process much easier.

INGREDIENTS

1 sheet of nori

200g cooked sushi rice (page 205)

3 slices of avocado

2½ crab sticks

1 cucumber baton, cut the same length as the nori sheet (peel and deseed the cucumber before cutting the baton)

1 tsp Japanese mayonnaise (good-quality mayonnaise with a touch of wasabi to taste will also work well)

1 tbsp white sesame seeds, toasted

As this is an inside-out roll (a roll with the rice on the outside), you must first fold the sheet of nori in half width-wise and cut it across the fold. Place one piece of the nori, shiny side down and with the long side facing towards you, on a piece of cling film and cover the entire piece with the rice. Allow the rice to extend out further than the edges of the nori at the top and bottom (not the sides).

Place your sushi mat on top and carefully flip the rice-covered sheet over onto the other side. The seaweed side should now face up. Don't worry if some rice falls away – just pat it back in place.

Remove the cling film, then spread the avocado slices, crab sticks and cucumber in a line across the width of the nori sheet at the edge closest to you, then lightly spread the mayonnaise on top of the ingredients.

To roll the sushi, fold the mat over, starting at the edge closest to you and tucking in the end of the nori to start the roll. Keep rolling, lifting up the mat as you go and keeping the pressure even but gentle until you have finished the roll. When the rice has been rolled, the two ends will seal as the rice binds together.

Place a dry pan on a low heat. Add the sesame seeds and stir constantly for 3–5 minutes, until they are lightly coloured. Remove the pan from the heat and transfer the seeds to a plate to cool completely. Be careful, as they will be very hot.

Roll the filled roll in the cooled toasted sesame seeds, then place on a board to dry out before cutting. The roll will firm up after 10 minutes; if you try to cut it any sooner, it will be too soft. Cut it into eight even-sized pieces with a wet, very sharp knife. If you don't use a sharp knife, the roll will be squashed as you cut it.

Arrange the pieces on a plate and serve.

ISO SALMON, AVOCADO & MASAGO MAKI

It is very important to make sure that the salmon is the freshest that you can get when making sushi. I usually tell our fishmonger here in Donnybrook Fair a few days in advance that I am making this dish, and I would suggest that you let your fishmonger know in advance so that he will have the freshest fish available for you on the day.

INGREDIENTS

1 sheet of nori

200g sushi rice, cooked (see opposite)

150g fresh salmon, finely chopped

3 slices of avocado

Japanese mayonnaise

masago (fish egg roe)

wasabi, to serve

As this is an inside-out roll (a roll with the rice on the outside), you must first fold the sheet of nori in half and split it in the middle. Place it shiny side down and with the long side facing towards you on a piece of cling film to help flip it over later and cover the entire piece of nori with the rice. Allow the rice to extend out further than the piece of nori at the top and bottom (not the sides).

Place your sushi mat on top and carefully flip the rice-covered sheet over onto the other side. The seaweed side should now face up. Remove the cling film, then place the salmon and avocado along the centre of the sheet and add some mayonnaise along the filling.

To roll the sushi, fold the mat over, starting at the edge closest to you and tucking in the end of the nori to start the roll. Keep rolling, lifting up the mat as you go and keeping the pressure even but gentle until you have finished the roll. When the maki has been rolled, the two ends will seal as the rice binds together.

Pat some masago into the rice on the outside for flavour and decoration. Rest on a board for 10 minutes, then cut into eight even slices and serve with wasabi.

MAKES
600G

SUSHI RICE

A great friend of mine who has built a successful sushi business in Dublin hosts our sushi classes at the Donnybrook Fair Cookery School. It's always fantastic to have an expert on hand. Did you know that some chefs train for seven years just to learn how to wash the rice correctly for this dish? I don't expect you to commit so much time to the task, of course, but do make sure you wash the rice really well in order to remove as much starch as possible. 250g of uncooked rice will increase to approximately 600g after cooking.

INGREDIENTS

250g sushi rice

325ml water (or as per instructions on the packet)

1 piece of kombu (optional)

2 tbsp sushi rice seasoning (page 195)

Wash the rice under cold running water until the water runs clear.

Put the rice in a saucepan with the water and kombu. Cover with a lid and bring to the boil, then remove the kombu, put the lid back on, turn the heat down and simmer for 10 minutes. Remove from the heat and let it sit for 10 minutes. Once you have removed the kombu, don't take the lid off the saucepan at any point.

Put the hot rice in a shallow dish and pour the sushi seasoning over the surface of the rice. Mix the seasoning into the rice with quick cutting strokes, preferably by using a spatula. Mix the seasoning in gently, though, as you don't want to break the grains of rice. The rice should look shiny and be at room temperature when you are ready to use it.

Vegetable
Sides

SERVES
6

PREPARE AHEAD VEGETABLES

A very popular class here at the cookery school in Donnybrook Fair is themed around fast cooking. With our busy lifestyles, the last thing we want to do is prepare vegetables for dinner every night. This process is a fantastic way of preparing vegetables ahead of time, allowing you to complete the cooking process in minutes in the evening. The order of preparing the vegetables is very important and keep in mind that they are to be cooked in order from lightest to darkest in colour. The reason for this is that the vegetables will colour the water and you don't want light green cauliflower!

INGREDIENTS

1 large cauliflower

1 head of broccoli

6 carrots

1 butternut squash

salt

Prepare the cauliflower by breaking the head into individual bite-sized florets. Prepare the broccoli in the same way. Peel the carrots and butternut squash and cut into bite-sized pieces.

Place a large pan of cold water on a high heat, season with salt and bring to the boil. Prepare a large bowl of iced water and set it beside you.

When the water is boiling, add the cauliflower florets and cook for 2–3 minutes. Remove from the pan with a slotted spoon and plunge into the iced water. When cool, remove from the iced water and set on kitchen paper to remove the excess water. This process sets the colour of the vegetables and ensures they keep their bright, vibrant colours on the plate.

Carry out the same process for the butternut squash, the carrots and finally the broccoli, in that order.

When all the vegetables are prepared, place them in an airtight container and put them in the fridge for up to four or five days. When you get home in the evening, simply place a large pan of water on a high heat. When the water is boiling, add the vegetables to heat through (this will take only 2–3 minutes), then remove them from the pan and serve immediately.

SERVES
4-6

CARAMELISED RED ONIONS

This is a very quick way to caramelise onions without cooking them for a very long time on a low heat. These are so versatile and will keep for up to two weeks in a sterilised jar in the fridge. I serve them with steak, burgers, salads, cold meats and cheese. They also make a great topping for pizzas.

INGREDIENTS

150ml water

1½ tbsp caster sugar

3 red onions, finely sliced

3 tbsp good-quality red wine vinegar

Place a large pan on a low heat and add the water, sugar and red onions.

Gently cook the onions for about 15–20 minutes, stirring regularly.

When the onions are soft, increase the heat to high. Add the red wine vinegar and let it bubble for a few minutes until most of the liquid has evaporated, before removing the pan from the heat. Allow to cool.

SERVES
4

ROASTED CHERRY TOMATOES

This is such a versatile dish and goes with pretty much everything. Keep a close eye on the tomatoes in the oven, as the ripeness of the tomatoes will influence the cooking time. You want to serve them just as they are starting to burst.

INGREDIENTS

500g cherry tomatoes on the vine

2 garlic cloves, grated

3 tbsp olive oil

pinch of flaky sea salt

Preheat the oven to 200°C/180°C fan/gas mark 6.

Place the tomatoes (still on the vine) and garlic in a bowl, then drizzle with the olive oil and season with salt. Toss well and pour into a roasting tray.

Roast in the oven for 20–30 minutes, until the tomatoes start to burst. Remove from the oven and serve.

BUTTERED CABBAGE

The technique used here is called blanching. This sets the colour and ensures a bright, vibrant green cabbage. This can be done earlier in the day and then finished when you're ready to serve dinner.

INGREDIENTS

1 large Savoy cabbage

25g butter

salt and freshly ground black pepper

Remove the stalk from the cabbage and shred the leaves finely.

Place a pot of salted water on a high heat and bring to the boil. Place a large bowl of iced water on the side.

Add the cabbage to the pot and boil for 1 minute, then drain and transfer to the iced water. When cool, drain the cabbage and set aside. Place the cabbage in an airtight container and put in the fridge. I usually do this a couple of hours before I need it and then just finish the dish, but it will keep for up to two days in the fridge.

To finish, place a pan on a medium heat and add the butter. When the butter has melted, add the cabbage and heat through for 2–3 minutes. Season with salt and pepper and serve.

SERVES
4

CRUSHED MINTED PEAS

Some frozen vegetable products are fantastic and you can't beat frozen peas. The peas are frozen at their very best, so I never use fresh peas.

INGREDIENTS

250g fresh or frozen peas

1 tbsp roughly chopped fresh mint leaves

10g butter

salt and freshly ground black pepper

Place a pan of salted water on a high heat and bring to the boil. Add the peas and boil rapidly with the lid off for 3–4 minutes. Remove from the heat and drain the peas, then transfer them to a food processor. Allow the peas to cool a little before you add the mint. If the peas are too hot, the mint will turn black.

Add the mint and butter and pulse to mix well. Don't process the peas too much, though, as this will turn them into a purée and you are looking for peas with texture.

Check for seasoning and adjust to taste with salt and pepper.

SERVES
4

HONEY-ROASTED CARROTS & PARSNIPS

Roasting is a magical way to cook vegetables. The roasting process dramatically heightens the flavour of the vegetables and brings them to a higher level. Although I love the carrot and parsnip combination in this recipe, you can use whatever vegetables you like to roast.

INGREDIENTS

3 tbsp olive oil

4 large parsnips

4 medium carrots

salt and freshly ground black pepper

2 tbsp clear honey

chopped fresh flat-leaf parsley, to garnish

Preheat the oven to 220°C/200°C fan/gas mark 7.

Add the oil to a large baking tray and place in the oven to heat up.

Peel the vegetables, making sure to also cut the parsnips in half lengthways and carefully remove the centre core. Cut the carrots in half lengthways and the parsnips in quarters lengthways.

Remove the tray from the oven and toss the vegetables in the hot oil, then season with salt and pepper.

Roast in the oven for 30–45 minutes, until tender. Remove from the oven, drizzle over the honey and stir well. Return to the oven for 5 minutes to heat through.

Remove from the oven and place in a warmed serving dish. Garnish with some freshly chopped parsley.

The Humble
Potato

SERVES
4-6

WARM POTATO SALAD

It may be hard to believe, but we run a very successful class here at the cookery school simply on potatoes. They are so versatile. This first recipe is a modern interpretation of a potato salad with no mayonnaise; it goes with almost everything. The secret to this salad is to allow the potatoes to air dry and cool so that they are just warm before you dress the salad and add the mint leaves. If the potatoes are too hot, the mint will turn black.

INGREDIENTS

750g baby potatoes

3–4 tbsp olive oil

pinch of fine sea salt

handful of fresh mint leaves, finely shredded

Place a pan of cold water on a high heat and season the water with a good sprinkling of salt. Add the potatoes and bring to the boil.

Reduce the heat to a gentle simmer and cook the potatoes for about 15 minutes, until just tender. Check that the potatoes are cooked by inserting a small knife into one – there should be no resistance and the potato should hold its shape.

Drain the potatoes into a colander to remove all the water and return to the empty pot to air dry for 5 minutes.

When still warm, dress the potatoes with the olive oil and season with a pinch of sea salt. Add the shredded fresh mint to the warm potatoes and serve.

SERVES
4

CRISPY POTATO WEDGES WITH ROSEMARY

These make a great alternative to chips, and since they are baked, they are also a healthier option. These are also handy if you get your timings a bit off, as you can take them out of the oven to slow down the roasting, then return them to the oven when you're back on track. You will still get a beautifully crunchy potato wedge.

INGREDIENTS

4 large Rooster potatoes (1 per person), washed and skin left on

2 garlic cloves, grated

2 tbsp olive oil

1 tbsp finely chopped fresh rosemary

coarse sea salt and freshly ground black pepper

Preheat the oven to 200°C/180°C fan/gas mark 6. Line a baking tray with non-stick baking paper.

Cut the potatoes into large wedges. Dry them really well with a clean cloth and place in a large bowl.

Add the remaining ingredients to the bowl and mix well, then tip the potatoes onto the lined tray.

Transfer the potatoes to the oven and bake for 45–50 minutes, until golden-brown and cooked all the way through. Turn them over halfway through the cooking time.

Serve the wedges hot from the oven.

SERVES
4

PERFECT MASH

When cooking potatoes for mash, there are no shortcuts. The potatoes must be placed in a large pan of cold water seasoned with salt. If they are placed in a pot of boiling water, the outsides cook too quickly and the insides will never quite cook through. This usually results in a lumpy mash.

INGREDIENTS

500g potatoes

50g butter

25ml milk

salt and freshly ground black pepper

For variations you can add the following:

1–2 tablespoons of wholegrain mustard after seasoning the mash with salt and pepper.

50g freshly grated Parmesan and a handful of chopped fresh flat-leaf parsley after seasoning the mash with salt and pepper.

3 whole, peeled garlic cloves to the potatoes at the beginning – leave in the potatoes when mashing. You can then add a handful of chopped fresh chives after seasoning the mash with salt and pepper.

25g grated strong red Cheddar when you mash the potatoes.

Try to choose potatoes that are all the same size. If there are smaller ones in the bag, then cut the larger potatoes to the same size as the smaller ones. Peel the potatoes and place in a large pot with plenty of room. Cover with cold water, making sure they're covered by at least 4cm of water. Add a couple of pinches of salt.

Place the pot on a high heat and bring to the boil, then reduce the heat and simmer gently. The cooking time will depend on the size of your potatoes, so check them after 15 minutes. The potatoes are cooked when they are still holding their shape but you can insert a small knife or skewer into the centre of the potato without resistance.

Drain the potatoes into a colander to remove all the water and return to the empty pot. Cover the pot with a clean, dry kitchen towel to air dry for 5 minutes.

Place the butter and milk in a separate small pot and gently bring to just below boiling point, then immediately remove the pot from the heat.

Mash the potatoes well with a potato masher. When they are completely smooth, slowly add the milk and butter mix, stirring really well with a spatula. Add enough of the liquid to create the desired consistency. It should just fall off the spatula with a little gentle persuasion.

Season with salt and pepper to taste and serve straight away.

SERVES 4

FRITES (SKINNY FRIES)

The very best chips are the ones that are cooked a number of times and at different temperatures, hence the term 'triple-fried chips'. These are the skinny variety, but the principle is exactly the same if you prefer chunkier chips.

INGREDIENTS

4 large potatoes, unpeeled (preferably Maris Piper, but Roosters will also work well)

vegetable oil, for deep frying

pinch of fine sea salt

Wash the potatoes well, then cut lengthways into thin discs. Cut each disc into thin chips and place in a bowl of cold water for 2–3 hours to remove as much starch as possible.

When you're ready to cook, preheat a deep fat fryer to 160°C. Drain the chips and dry well with kitchen paper or a clean kitchen towel.

When the vegetable oil in the deep fat fryer is hot, add the chips. Don't overcrowd the fryer, so do this in two batches if necessary. Fry the chips for 2–3 minutes, until they begin to take on a little colour. Lift out of the oil and allow to cool in the basket over the oil.

When cool, return to the oil and fry until the chips have taken on a little more colour. They should be pale and they should still look uncooked. Transfer to a tray while you repeat the process for the second batch.

Increase the temperature of the oil to 180°C.

Just before serving, add the two batches together and quickly fry until golden. Transfer to some kitchen paper to remove any excess oil, season well with sea salt and serve straight away.

POTATO DAUPHINOISE

This is the perfect potato to serve for any dinner party because you can make this dish the day before and then reheat it just before serving. It takes so much pressure off to have some dishes prepared well in advance (and it helps that nobody can tell the difference!).

INGREDIENTS

60g butter

1kg Maris Piper potatoes

150ml double cream

150ml milk

2 garlic cloves, grated

salt and freshly ground black pepper

Preheat the oven to 160°C/140°C fan/gas mark 3.

Melt half of the butter, then brush a 20cm fixed-bottom cake tin very lightly with the melted butter, as this helps the baking paper to stick to the tin. Line the tin with non-stick baking paper. You can do this by cutting two rectangles of paper that are the same width as the tin and long enough to come just above the height of the sides. Don't worry if the joins at the corners aren't completely flush.

Peel the potatoes and slice them thinly, close to the thickness of a €1 coin. Immediately place the potatoes in a bowl of cold water.

Heat the cream, milk and garlic in a medium pot to just before the boiling point, then remove from the heat.

Drain the potatoes and dry them well. Arrange the slices in overlapping layers until they cover the base of the tin and season with salt and pepper. Repeat until all the potatoes are in the tin, seasoning each layer as you go.

Gently pour the warm liquid over the potatoes until they are almost covered. Don't worry if you don't use all the liquid.

Dot the top with small knobs of the remaining butter. Place the tin in the oven and bake for 1–1¼ hours.

Check that the potatoes are cooked by inserting a small knife or skewer into the potatoes – you shouldn't feel any resistance.

Remove from the oven and allow the potatoes to firm up before removing them from the tin. Cut the potatoes into six to eight portions and serve.

If you are making this in advance, allow the potatoes to cool completely in the tin. Wrap tightly in cling film and refrigerate overnight.

A couple of hours before you're ready to serve, remove the tin from the fridge and gently remove the potatoes from the tin by lifting out the baking paper. Divide into six to eight portions and place on a baking tray lined with non-stick baking paper.

Preheat the oven to 200°C/180°C fan/gas mark 6. Transfer the tray to the oven for 12–15 minutes, until the portions are heated through. They will then be ready to serve.

ROAST POTATOES

Perfectly roasted, golden-brown potatoes are the perfect accompaniment for roast meats. As with the frites on page 225, the best results are achieved by cooking the potatoes more than once. This will give them a golden, crisp exterior and a wonderfully fluffy interior.

INGREDIENTS

8 medium Maris Piper potatoes

4 tbsp duck or goose fat (if you don't have either of these, use vegetable oil)

salt and freshly ground black pepper

4 garlic cloves, unpeeled

4 sprigs of fresh thyme

Try to choose potatoes that are all the same size so that they will cook in the same amount of time. Peel the potatoes and cut each one into quarters. Place in a pan with plenty of room, cover with cold water and add a good pinch of salt. Bring to the boil, then reduce the heat and simmer for 2–3 minutes. Drain well, then return the potatoes to the pot and cover the pot with a clean kitchen towel.

Preheat the oven to 200°C/180°C fan/gas mark 6.

Place the fat or oil in a baking tray large enough to fit the potatoes in one layer with space around them. Place the tray in the oven for 10 minutes to heat the fat/oil.

Remove the towel and gently shake the pot to rough up the edges of the potatoes. Don't be too aggressive, though.

Carefully remove the baking tray from the oven and add the potatoes to the hot fat. Using a spoon, gently turn the potatoes over to coat them in the fat. Season well with salt and pepper, then scatter the garlic and thyme around the potatoes and return the tray to the oven.

Roast for 45–60 minutes, turning the potatoes over halfway through the cooking time to ensure the potatoes are golden all over.

Remove from the oven and transfer to a serving dish. Include the garlic cloves, as they will now be beautifully sweet from the roasting when squeezed out of their skins.

The Art
of Sauces

SWEET CHILLI SAUCE

Sauces can elevate any dish and, contrary to popular perception, are really easy to make. This sauce is unlike the thick version you buy in bottles – it is light and zingy.

INGREDIENTS

1 red pepper, deseeded and
  finely chopped

1 red chilli, deseeded and
  finely chopped

100g caster sugar

100ml rice wine vinegar

100ml water

Place all the ingredients in a pan. Bring to the boil, then reduce the heat and leave to simmer for 20–30 minutes. Taste a piece of pepper to check if it is cooked enough – it should be soft on the outside but still firm in the middle.

Allow the mixture to cool, then place it in a food processor and blend until smooth.

Return to the pan and cook until it's slightly sticky, which should take about 20 minutes more. It will then be ready to serve. This can be stored in the fridge in a sterilised airtight jar for up to six months (see the Jams and Chutneys chapter for instructions on how to sterilise jars).

TARTAR SAUCE

One of my favourite food heroes maintains that you don't have to make absolutely everything yourself from scratch. This simple sauce is a good example of that, as it combines shop-bought produce with fresh ingredients. Tartar sauce goes well with fried fish as well as cold fish and shellfish.

INGREDIENTS

2 tbsp gherkins

2 tbsp capers

200ml good-quality mayonnaise

1 shallot, finely diced

3 tbsp chopped fresh flat-leaf
  parsley

salt and freshly ground black
  pepper

freshly squeezed lemon juice,
  to taste

Drain, rinse and finely chop the gherkins and capers.

Place the mayonnaise, shallot, parsley, capers and gherkins in a bowl and mix well. Season with salt and pepper and add lemon juice to taste.

CREAMY MINT SAUCE

The art of making sauces is quite simple and this sauce is a great introduction. Mint sauce goes really well with baked ham or lamb. Once you have mastered the technique, you can get creative with different herbs, such as fresh chives, tarragon or sage.

INGREDIENTS

vegetable oil

1 small onion, finely diced

150ml white wine

400ml vegetable stock

300ml single cream

small handful of fresh mint leaves

salt and freshly ground black pepper

Heat a splash of vegetable oil in a frying pan set over a medium heat. Add the chopped onion and sweat for 3–4 minutes, until soft. Don't allow the onion to colour.

Increase the heat and add the wine. Allow to reduce to about a one-third of its original volume. Add the stock and reduce again to one-third of the original volume.

Pour in the cream and simmer for 2–3 minutes. Once the desired consistency is achieved, remove the pan from the heat and allow to cool, then chop the mint leaves and stir them into the sauce (if you add the mint when the sauce is still hot, it will turn black).

Season with salt and freshly ground black pepper and serve straight away.

SERVES
4–6

SPICED PLUM SAUCE

This is a great sauce to serve with the Asian fillet of pork on page 125, but it's equally good with the simple roast duck on page 134.

INGREDIENTS

300g ripe red plums

1 tbsp olive oil

20g shallot, finely chopped

1 tsp Chinese five spice

50ml red wine

75g dark brown sugar

250ml beef stock

To peel the plums, bring a pot of water to the boil, then reduce the heat to a simmer. Cut a small X in the bottom of the plums and place in the water. When the skin begins to blister, remove from the pot and transfer to a bowl of cold water. When cool, remove the skin and the stones and cut into quarters.

Place a pan on a medium heat. When it's hot, add the olive oil and then the shallot. Reduce the heat and cook for 3–4 minutes, until the shallot is soft but not coloured. Add the Chinese five spice and cook for 1 minute more.

Increase the heat and add the red wine. Cook until the volume of wine has reduced by half.

Add the plums, sugar and stock and let the mix simmer for 5–10 minutes, depending on the ripeness of the fruit, until the plums are cooked through. Be careful that you don't overcook the plums – they should hold their shape.

Remove the plums with a slotted spoon and let the sauce bubble away until it thickens to a sauce consistency, which should take about 5 minutes more.

Reduce the heat to low, then return the plums to the sauce to warm through.

SERVES 4

CREAM OF MUSHROOM SAUCE

This is the ultimate comfort sauce and I usually serve it with steak or chicken. Use a variety of mushrooms for flavour and texture, but the sauce will also work well if you only have one type of mushroom in the larder.

INGREDIENTS

15g butter

1 tbsp olive oil

250g mixed mushrooms, cleaned and sliced

100ml brandy

250ml chicken stock

225ml cream

salt and freshly ground black pepper

2 tbsp chopped fresh flat-leaf parsley

Place a frying pan on a high heat and add the butter and oil. When the oil and butter have melted together, add the mushrooms and fry for 2–3 minutes, until soft. Take the pan off the heat and remove the mushrooms from the pan.

Reduce the heat to medium. Return the frying pan to the heat, add the brandy and scrape the base of the pan to release the juices. Ignite the brandy in order to burn off the alcohol (this technique is called flambé).

When the brandy has stopped flaming, add the stock and reduce the brandy and stock to one-third of its initial volume. Then add the cream and simmer for 2–3 minutes to allow the sauce to thicken.

Season with salt and pepper, then return the mushrooms to the sauce to warm through. Stir in the parsley and serve straight away.

CARAMEL SAUCE

This is another classic sauce, one that goes brilliantly with many desserts. The secret to this sauce is to watch the caramelisation of the sugar and butter very carefully. The difference between a beautiful caramel and a burnt caramel is only a matter of seconds. And don't use a non-stick pan, as it's difficult to judge the caramelisation in a dark pan.

INGREDIENTS

100g caster sugar

75g butter, cut into small cubes and softened

1 vanilla pod, split in half lengthways and seeds scraped out

200ml double cream

Place the sugar, butter and vanilla seeds and pod in a pan set over a low heat and allow everything to melt together.

Continue to cook on a low heat for 2–3 minutes, stirring with a heatproof spatula until the mix turns a golden caramel colour.

Remove from the heat and add the cream. Be careful, as it may spit. Quickly stir to combine everything.

Increase the heat to medium and return the pot to the heat. Cook for 5 minutes, stirring all the time.

Remove from the heat and allow to cool, removing the vanilla pod before serving.

The Great
DF Bake Off

SERVES 8-10

AFTERNOON CITRUS TEA CAKE

During classes in the cookery school, I'm often asked how to make a really quick cake. This recipe is super fast, especially if you have a food processor. It also works with a standard food mixer, although it takes a little longer to mix, and it can be done by hand with a little elbow grease. For variation, you can substitute the orange with lemon.

INGREDIENTS

175g caster sugar

115g butter, softened

2 medium eggs

1½ tsp vanilla extract

170g self-raising flour

pinch of salt

zest and juice of 1 large orange

2 tbsp orange yogurt

Preheat the oven to 180°C/160°C fan/gas mark 4. Place a 1lb baking parchment tin liner in a loaf tin. If you can't get the liners, lightly oil the loaf tin and line with non-stick baking paper instead.

Place 115g of the caster sugar and all of the butter in a food processor or mixer and beat until light and creamy. Beat in the eggs one at a time, until well incorporated each time. Add the vanilla extract and beat well.

Sift the flour and salt together, then beat into the butter and sugar mix. Beat in the orange zest and the yogurt.

Spoon the cake batter into the lined 1lb loaf tin and bake in the oven for 40–45 minutes. You will know that the cake is done when you insert a skewer into the centre of the cake and it comes out clean. Remove from the oven and leave in the tin to cool.

Pierce the top of the cake all over with a cocktail stick. Make sure to pierce deep down into the cake itself.

Place the orange juice (you should have about 60ml) and the remaining 60g of caster sugar in a pan and set on a medium heat. When the sugar has dissolved, increase the heat to high and boil for 1 minute. Remove from the heat.

While the cake is still warm, spoon the orange sugar syrup over the entire top of the cake. The holes created will allow the syrup to moisten the cake.

CHERRY & ALMOND BUNDT CAKE

Bundt cakes are ring-shaped cakes with a hole in the centre. The shape is inspired by a traditional European cake, although the tins were first developed in the United States. The cake is baked in a Bundt cake tin, available from all good kitchen shops. It's a great way to present any cake, as it looks so dramatic on a cake stand.

INGREDIENTS

175g softened butter, plus extra for greasing

225g self-raising flour, plus extra for dusting

200g glacé cherries

175g caster sugar

zest of 1 lemon

3 large free-range eggs

2 tbsp natural yogurt

50g ground almonds

For the decoration:

15g flaked almonds

175g icing sugar, sifted

juice of 1 lemon

4 glacé cherries, left whole

Preheat the oven to 180°C/160°C fan/gas mark 4. Brush a 23cm Bundt tin with melted butter and dust with flour, shaking out any excess flour.

Cut the cherries into quarters, place in a sieve and pour boiling water over them to remove the syrup. Drain well, then dry the cherries thoroughly on kitchen paper. Place the cherries in a small bowl and toss in 2 tablespoons of the flour.

Place the sugar, butter and lemon zest in a large bowl and beat until light and fluffy.

Beat the eggs in one at a time until well incorporated into the butter and sugar, then beat the yogurt into the mix.

Gently fold in the ground almonds and the remaining flour, then fold the cherries into the batter.

Pour the cake batter into the prepared tin. Bake in the oven for 35–40 minutes, until well risen and golden-brown, and a skewer inserted into the centre comes out clean. Leave to cool in the tin for 10 minutes, then turn out and cool completely on a wire rack.

While the cake is cooling, toast the almonds. Place a dry pan on a low heat and add the flaked almonds, stirring every 15–20 seconds until they begin to take on a very light colour. Remove from the heat and transfer to a plate to cool.

To make the icing, mix the icing sugar with the lemon juice to a thick paste. The icing should be a consistency that will slowly drizzle down the sides of the cake. If it's too firm, add a little more lemon juice. If it's too loose, add a little more icing sugar.

Spoon the icing over the cooled cake. It should begin to ease down the sides of the cake. Place the whole cherries on the top of the cake at regular intervals.

Sprinkle the toasted almonds around the top of the cake and set aside to allow the icing to firm up.

MAKES
12

LEMON MADELEINES

These classic little French cakes are perfect for tea or coffee. I also use them with desserts. They are best eaten on the day, although they will keep in an airtight container for a few days, but they never last that long!

INGREDIENTS

100g caster sugar

2 medium eggs

100g unsalted butter, melted and cooled, plus extra for greasing

zest and juice of 1 unwaxed lemon

100g plain flour, plus extra for dusting

¾ tsp baking powder

Place the sugar and eggs in a bowl and beat until light and fluffy. Add the melted butter and the lemon zest and juice and mix well.

Sift the flour and baking powder together, then gently fold into the wet mix to form a batter.

Cover the bowl with cling film and leave to rest in the fridge for about 30 minutes.

Preheat the oven to 200°C/180°C fan/gas mark 6. Brush a 12-hole madeleine tin lightly with some melted butter and dust with flour, shaking out any excess flour.

Remove the batter from the fridge and spoon even amounts into each hole of the madeleine tin. Bake in the oven for 8–10 minutes, until the madeleines are golden and fully cooked.

Remove from the oven and allow to cool before carefully removing from the tin.

MAKES
12

ROCK BUNS

We all have to start somewhere, and rock buns are a great introduction to baking. These are quick to assemble and bake, so this is an ideal recipe for those times when unexpected guests call over.

INGREDIENTS

225g self-raising flour

1 tsp baking powder

110g butter, cubed and
  softened

110g mixed dried fruit

55g currants

55g granulated sugar

1½ tsp mixed spice

1 medium egg

2–3 tbsp milk

2 tsp vanilla extract

Demerara sugar, for sprinkling

Preheat the oven to 180°C/160°C fan/gas mark 4. Line a baking tray with non-stick baking paper.

Sift the flour and baking powder into a large bowl. Add the softened butter and lightly rub the mixture together with your fingertips until it resembles fine breadcrumbs. Add the mixed dried fruit, currants, sugar and mixed spice, stirring until all the ingredients are well incorporated.

Mix the egg with 2 tablespoons of milk and the vanilla extract in a separate small bowl, then add to the dry ingredients and mix to create a stiff dough. If the mix looks a little dry, then add the remaining tablespoon of milk. The dough should hold its shape when placed on the baking sheet.

Divide the mixture into twelve even ball-shaped buns and place on the lined baking tray. Leave some room around them, as they will spread a little as they bake.

Sprinkle the top of the buns with the demerara sugar and bake in the oven for 15–20 minutes, until golden-brown. Remove from the oven and allow to cool on a wire rack. These are best eaten on the day that they are made, but can be kept in an airtight container for a day or two and reheated in the oven.

MAKES
12

PORTUGUESE CUSTARD TARTS

No matter how hard I've tried, no Portuguese bakery has ever divulged the secret to making these tarts. Each bakery has its own unique version of these fabulous tarts, so I decided to create my own. I use a rough puff pastry and vanilla custard. If you don't have time to make the puff pastry from scratch, then shop-bought will work — just make sure it's an all-butter version.

INGREDIENTS

125g caster sugar

3 large free-range egg yolks

30g cornflour

225ml double cream

175ml full-fat milk

vanilla pod, split, seeds scraped out

Icing sugar for dusting

For the rough puff pastry:

115g plain flour, plus extra for dusting

large pinch of salt

115g cold butter, cut into small cubes, plus extra for greasing

2–3 tbsp cold water

1 small egg whisked with 1 tsp cold water, for the egg wash

To make the rough puff pastry, sift the flour and salt into a food processor and add the cold butter. Pulse to create a mix that still has large pieces of butter visible, about the size of a 1 cent coin.

Add 2 tablespoons of the water to the flour and butter mixture and pulse until it starts to come together. You only want to add just enough cold water to form a dough when you squeeze it together in your hands. Be careful not to add too much water. Add the remaining tablespoon if needed.

Flour the work surface well and tip the dough out onto it. Roll the dough out to a rectangle approximately 38 x 20cm.

With the rectangle facing away from you lengthways, fold one-third of the dough from the top to the centre, then fold the other third from the bottom over that. It's very important to brush off any excess flour before each fold. Press down with the rolling pin in the centre, the top and the bottom, then wrap in cling film and chill for 30 minutes.

Remove from the fridge, unwrap and roll the pastry out again in the opposite direction to the same 38 x 20cm proportions. Fold in exactly the same way as before. This is creating the layers of the puff pastry. Wrap in cling film again and chill for 30 minutes.

Repeat this process three or four more times, continuing to turn, roll and brush off the excess flour before each fold. After the last folding stage, wrap the pastry in cling film and place in the fridge to chill for several hours or, preferably, overnight.

To make the vanilla custard, beat the sugar and the egg yolks in a medium bowl until light and creamy. Sift the cornflour into the egg mix and beat until well mixed.

Heat the cream, milk, vanilla seeds and pod in a medium pot to just under boiling point, then remove from the heat. Whisk about one-third of the heated milk and cream into the egg and cornflour mix and then pour the custard back into the pan with the rest of the cream and milk.

Return the pan to a medium heat and continue to stir the custard continuously until it thickens. Be careful not to boil the custard as this will cause it to split. When thickened remove the pan from the heat and transfer the custard to a clean bowl and cover its surface with cling film to prevent a skin from forming. Allow to cool completely, then remove the vanilla pod.

Remove the pastry from the fridge and allow to rest at room temperature for 15–20 minutes.

Preheat the oven to 200°C/180°C fan/gas mark 6. Lightly brush six wells of a 12–hole bun tin with some melted butter.

Dust the work surface with icing sugar and roll the pastry out, until it's 3–5mm thick. Using a 10cm pastry cutter, cut six discs from the rolled pastry. Gently press the pastry discs into the greased bun tin. Divide the cooled custard between the six pastry cases. Brush the edges of the pastry lightly with a little egg wash.

Bake the tarts in the oven for 25–30 minutes, until the pastry is golden and the custard has taken on a golden colour too. Allow the tarts to cool in the tin before serving.

COFFEE AND WALNUT CAKE

As in previous recipes in the book, the walnuts are roasted to improve the texture but also to heighten the walnut flavour. The icing is beautifully soft, so once iced, you should chill the cake for about 1 hour before serving.

INGREDIENTS

100g walnut halves

225g butter, softened, plus extra for greasing

340g self-raising flour, plus extra for dusting

225g caster sugar

1 tsp vanilla extract

4 large free-range eggs

2 tbsp vanilla yogurt

2 tsp instant coffee granules

For the icing:

500g icing sugar

125g butter, cut into small cubes and softened

125g mascarpone

1 tsp vanilla extract

2 tsp instant coffee granules

Preheat the oven to 220°C/200°C fan/gas mark 7.

Place the walnuts on a baking tray and roast for 5–10 minutes, watching carefully so they don't burn. You will know they are ready when they release a beautiful walnut aroma. Remove them from the oven and allow to cool. Hold back eight for the decoration and roughly chop the remainder.

Reduce the oven temperature to 180°C/160°C fan/gas mark 4. Line the bases of two 20cm loose-bottomed sponge tins with non-stick baking paper. Brush the sides with melted butter and dust with flour, shaking out any excess.

Beat the butter, sugar and vanilla extract until light, pale and fluffy. Beat in the eggs one at a time, beating well after each addition.

Sift the flour and fold it gently into the butter and sugar with a spatula. Gently stir in the yogurt.

Dissolve the coffee granules in 1 tablespoon of boiling water, then stir this into the batter and gently fold in the chopped walnuts.

Divide the cake batter between the two tins and lightly smooth the tops. Bake in the oven for 20–25 minutes. The cake should be springy to the touch and a skewer inserted into the centre should come out clean.

Cool in the tin for 15–20 minutes to firm up, then transfer to a wire rack to cool completely.

To make the icing, sift the icing sugar into a bowl, add the butter and beat until well combined. It won't come together like a traditional icing and will look very dry, but don't worry. Add the mascarpone and vanilla extract and beat until smooth. Dissolve the instant coffee in 2 teaspoons of boiling water and pour into the icing, beating well to mix.

Sandwich the two sponges together with a generous layer of the icing. Place on a cake stand or serving platter and cover the top and sides of the cake with the remaining icing. Don't try to make everything really smooth – freehand swirls give the cake great character. Decorate the top with the eight reserved walnuts.

Chocolate
Heaven

SERVES
4

CHICKEN MOLE

This is a beautifully fragrant stew inspired by the cuisine of Mexico. The addition of the chocolate creates a sauce that is rich, glossy and velvety brown. It tastes amazing and nobody guesses there is chocolate in the sauce. I serve this with long-grain rice.

INGREDIENTS

2 ripe tomatoes, peeled and finely chopped

vegetable oil

4 chicken fillets, cut into bite-sized pieces

1 large onion, finely sliced

2 garlic cloves, grated

1–2 green chillies (depending on how spicy you like it), deseeded and very finely chopped

2 tsp ground cumin

1½ tsp ground cinnamon

1 x 400g tin of chopped tomatoes

1 x 400g tin of red kidney beans, drained and rinsed

400ml chicken stock

pinch of caster sugar (optional)

80g dark chocolate (minimum 70% cocoa solids)

pinch of salt

cooked long-grain rice, to serve

lime wedges, to serve

8 tbsp sour cream, to serve

Preheat the oven to 170°C/150°C fan/gas mark 3.

You need to peel the tomatoes, so first bring a pot of water to the boil, then reduce the heat to a simmer. Have a bowl of iced water on the side. Remove the core of each tomato by inserting a small knife into the tomato at a slight angle, just deep enough to remove the core, and cutting in a circle. Then cut a small X in the bottom of the tomato. Carefully place the tomatoes in the pot of simmering water. Once the skin begins to lift away from the X, remove the tomatoes with a slotted spoon and place in the bowl of iced water. Once the tomatoes are cool, the skin will peel off easily and you can finely chop them.

Heat a light drizzle of vegetable oil in a large heavy-based casserole set on a medium heat, then add the chicken and fry for 4–5 minutes, until lightly browned. Don't crowd the pan, as the chicken will steam and not fry, so it might be better to do this in batches. Remove from the pot and set aside.

Add the onion, garlic and chillies and fry gently for 3–4 minutes, until lightly browned. Add the spices and fry for a couple of minutes more, until they become fragrant.

Add the fresh and tinned tomatoes, kidney beans and stock. Scrape all the caramelised pieces from the bottom of the pan to boost the flavour of the sauce.

Taste the sauce after it has been simmering for 5–10 minutes. Some tinned tomatoes are quite acidic, so if that's the case here, add half a teaspoon of sugar, check again and add a little more if required. Be careful, however, as just a little sugar will make a big difference.

Add 50g of the chocolate and then return the chicken to the pot. Bring to a simmer and place in the oven, covered with a lid, for 90 minutes.

Remove from the oven and check the seasoning. Add a little salt if required. Stir in the remaining chocolate and set aside to rest for 5–10 minutes.

Serve with long-grain rice, lime wedges and 2 table-spoons of sour cream per serving.

CLASSIC CHOCOLATE MOUSSE

Everyone loves the chocolate classes here at the cookery school. This dessert in particular is a student favourite. It's a wonderfully rich mousse, so a little goes a long way. There are endless variations on this, so you can select a flavoured chocolate if you like, such as orange or mint. Just make sure the chocolate is very good quality.

INGREDIENTS

115g dark chocolate (minimum 70% cocoa solids), broken into small pieces

55g butter, cubed and softened

4 free-range eggs, separated and at room temperature

70g icing sugar

300ml double cream

Place the chocolate and butter in a large heatproof bowl set over a pan of barely simmering water (a bain marie), making sure the bottom of the bowl doesn't touch the water. Stir well until melted, then set aside to cool.

When the chocolate and butter mix feels barely warm to the touch, add the egg yolks one at a time and mix well, then sift in the icing sugar and stir well.

In a spotlessly clean, dry, large bowl, whisk the egg whites until they form soft peaks.

In a separate bowl, whisk the double cream until soft peaks form.

Fold the double cream into the chocolate mixture, then fold in the egg whites very gently so as not to knock out all the air.

Pour the mousse into one large serving bowl or individual serving glasses, cover with cling film and transfer to the fridge overnight to set.

CHOCOLATE FONDANT WITH MIXED BERRY COMPOTE

Those of you who watch MasterChef will have seen the ambitions of many a budding chef come to a shuddering halt as they got their timings wrong and produced a chocolate cake and not a soft-centred fondant, so make sure to watch the timings carefully when making this recipe. This is a regular at the team-building classes we run here at the cookery school. For added fun I sometimes omit the cooking times from the recipe and the teams have to work it out for themselves.

INGREDIENTS

melted butter, for greasing

cocoa powder, for dusting

100g dark couverture chocolate

100g butter, cubed

2 eggs

2 egg yolks

50g caster sugar

75g plain flour, sifted

freshly whipped cream, to serve

For the mixed berry compote:

1 punnet of blueberries

2 tbsp caster sugar

1 tbsp water

1 punnet of raspberries

Brush eight 150ml dariole moulds with melted butter in an upwards direction and dust with cocoa powder. Place on a baking tray.

Melt the chocolate and butter in a heatproof bowl set over a small saucepan of barely simmering water (a bain marie), making sure the bottom of the bowl doesn't touch the water. Remove from the heat and allow to cool once the mix has melted.

Beat the eggs, egg yolks and sugar in a food mixer on high speed until light and creamy. Add the cooled chocolate mixture to the eggs and fold together, then fold in the sifted flour and mix until smooth.

Using a piping bag, fill the moulds until they are three-quarters full and place in the fridge until you're almost ready to serve.

Meanwhile, to make the mixed berry compote, place the blueberries in a pot with the sugar and water. Place on a medium heat and cook for 2–3 minutes, until the fruit softens and begins to pop. Remove from the heat, add the raspberries and set aside to cool.

When you're almost ready to serve the fondants, preheat the oven to 180°C/160°C fan/gas mark 4.

Bake in the oven for about 8–10 minutes. The cooking time may vary due to the consistency of the mix, so watch carefully. You will know that the fondants are cooked when they rise up, a firm crust has formed, they are just beginning to come away from the sides of the dariole moulds and the filling has just started to ooze out the top.

Remove from the oven and leave to sit for 1 minute. Run a small knife down the sides of the dariole moulds, then gently tip the fondant out into your hand and place upright on a serving plate.

Serve immediately (as the fondants will continue to cook as they sit and you want the middle to still be molten) with the mixed berry compote and some freshly whipped cream.

MAKES 24

CHERRY AND MIXED NUT CHOCOLATE BROWNIES

I don't think I have ever met anyone who doesn't like brownies. This recipe combines the richness of the chocolate with the sharpness of the cherries and the crunch of the nuts. A little tip I picked up recently from one of the students here at the cookery school was to add coffee to the chocolate, as it intensifies the chocolate flavour. So while you might think this a little odd, it's certainly worth giving it a try.

INGREDIENTS

300g unsalted butter, cut into small cubes

300g dark cooking chocolate (minimum 70% cocoa solids), broken into pieces

5 large eggs

450g granulated sugar

2 tbsp coffee granules

1 tbsp vanilla extract

200g plain flour

1 tsp salt

150g dried cherries

150g Donnybrook Fair luxury nut mix (pistachios, almonds, walnuts and pecans)

Preheat the oven to 180°C/160°C fan/gas mark 4. Line a 33 x 23 x 2.5cm baking tin with non-stick baking paper.

Melt the butter and chocolate together in a heatproof bowl set over a saucepan of barely simmering water (a bain marie), making sure the bottom of the bowl doesn't touch the water. Once the butter and chocolate have melted, remove from the heat and allow to cool a little.

Beat the eggs, sugar, coffee granules and vanilla extract together in a separate bowl until the mixture is thick and creamy and coats the back of a spoon. When cool to the touch, beat the melted chocolate mixture into the egg mixture.

Sift the flour and salt together, then add them to the batter and continue to beat until smooth. Stir in the dried cherries and nuts, then pour into the lined tin, making sure the mixture is evenly distributed in the tin.

Bake in the oven for 20–25 minutes, until the top has formed a light brown crust all over that has started to crack. Remove from the oven and allow to cool on a wire rack before cutting into squares.

WHITE HOT CHOCOLATE FOR GROWN-UPS

We stock an amazing array of artisan chocolate in the Donnybrook Fair stores, many from Irish chocolatiers. These artisan products combined with a recent visit to Krakow inspired this version of hot chocolate, as whenever I travel, I'm always looking for inspiration for classes in the cookery school.

INGREDIENTS

650ml milk

225ml double cream

1 cinnamon stick

100g good-quality vanilla white chocolate, broken into small pieces

100ml Mozart Chocolate Cream liqueur

Place the milk, double cream and cinnamon stick in a pan and gently heat to just below boiling.

Place the chocolate pieces in a tall measuring jug. Remove the cinnamon stick from the milk and pour the hot milk over the chocolate. Add the chocolate liqueur and blend with a hand-held blender until well mixed and frothy.

Pour into four tall glasses and serve straight away.

SERVES
8

CHOCOLATE ROULADE

The secret of success in gluten-free cooking is to create a dish that everybody loves, even those without an intolerance to gluten. This recipe appears in many of our classes and has changed many students' perceptions of gluten-free baking. You can vary the fruit – all soft fruits work really well with this.

INGREDIENTS

For the sponge base:

200g dark chocolate (minimum 70% cocoa solids)

5 large eggs, separated

140g caster sugar

icing sugar, for dusting

For the filling:

150ml double cream

200ml Greek yogurt

2 punnets of raspberries

Preheat the oven to 180°C/160°C fan/gas mark 4. Line a 33 x 25cm baking tray with non-stick baking paper.

Melt the chocolate in a heatproof bowl set over a saucepan of barely simmering water (a bain marie), making sure the bottom of the bowl doesn't touch the water. Set aside to cool.

Using an electric whisk, beat the egg whites in a spotlessly clean, dry bowl until stiff peaks form.

In a separate large bowl, whisk the egg yolks with the sugar until thick and pale, then fold in the melted chocolate.

Using a spatula, quickly stir in one-third of the egg whites to loosen the mixture, then gently fold in the remaining two-thirds.

Pour the mixture into the lined tray, spreading it out in an even layer, and bake in the oven for 15 minutes, until springy to the touch. Cover immediately with a damp cloth to prevent it from cracking and set aside to cool completely. When cool, remove the cloth from the sponge. Lift it out of the tin, keeping it on the baking paper.

To make the filling, lightly whip the cream and mix with the yogurt. Spread the whipped cream over the sponge, staying 1.25cm inside the edge of the base. Sprinkle the raspberries over the cream mixture.

Starting with a long side, roll up the sponge firmly, using the paper to help you. It's essential to keep the roll very tight. Wrap in non-stick baking paper and chill before serving. Serve dusted with icing sugar.

Glorious
Desserts

SERVES
6

SPICED BERRY, MAPLE SYRUP & VANILLA RICE PUDDING

If you like rice pudding, you will really love this version. If you don't normally like rice pudding, I encourage you to try this one, as it just might change your mind.

INGREDIENTS

200g Arborio rice

60g unsalted butter

600ml cold water

4 green cardamom pods, lightly crushed

2 cloves

1 cinnamon stick

½ vanilla pod, split in half lengthways

100g mascarpone

75ml maple syrup

2 tbsp icing sugar

150g raspberries

150g blueberries

Place the rice in a medium-sized pot with a tight-fitting lid along with the butter, water, cardamom, cloves, cinnamon stick and vanilla pod. Bring to the boil, then reduce the heat and simmer for 10–12 minutes, covered, until the rice is cooked al dente, which means it should be soft on the outside but still a little firm on the inside when you test a grain of rice.

Remove the pot from the heat, then retrieve the cardamom pods, cloves, cinnamon stick and vanilla pod and discard them.

Stir in the mascarpone, maple syrup and icing sugar, then gently stir in the berries.

Replace the lid and leave to rest for 5 minutes, then serve while still warm.

SERVES
6-8

JELLY & ICE CREAM

I often smile when chefs say that they are a bit embarrassed about using a recipe that isn't really a recipe, and while I feel that way about this recipe, I'm sure it will bring back happy memories of your own childhood and Sunday lunches.

INGREDIENTS

270g good-quality vanilla ice cream

1 x 135g block of flavoured jelly (whichever flavour you prefer)

Remove the ice cream from the freezer and leave it to sit at room temperature for about 30 minutes to soften it a little.

Cut the jelly into very small cubes. Dissolve the jelly in half the amount of water that the packet instructions suggest (you need to follow this step very carefully in order for the ice cream to set). Set aside to cool until it's just warm.

Beat the softened ice cream until well mixed, then slowly beat in the cooled jelly mix.

When completely mixed, transfer to a serving bowl and place in the fridge for 2–3 hours to set.

Additional Option:

For children's parties, you can make rainbow jelly and ice cream. This involves layering different flavours to create a rainbow effect. I usually use three different flavours: lemon, lime and strawberry. Make one flavour at a time and remember to allow each layer to set before adding the next layer on top of the first. Serve in clear plastic cups so the children can see the different layers.

SUMMER BERRY PUDDING WITH VANILLA ICE CREAM

This is a much-loved classic. Make sure you properly soak the bread so that the colour is uniform when serving. I use a bread tin but you can use any shape of tin that you like.

INGREDIENTS

1kg mixed summer berries, such as strawberries, blueberries, raspberries, blackberries, redcurrants and/or blackcurrants

250g caster sugar

2 tbsp water

1 large unsliced loaf of white bread or thickly sliced white bread, preferably slightly stale

1 x 500ml tub of good-quality vanilla ice cream

Line a 1lb loaf tin with a double layer of cling film.

Place the strawberries, blueberries, redcurrants and blackcurrants in a pan with the sugar and water and bring to the boil. Cook for 2–3 minutes, until the berries have just softened and are beginning to burst. Remove from the heat and add the raspberries and blackberries.

Cut the crusts off the loaf, then cut the loaf into medium-thick slices along the length of the bread so that you have long slices rather than square slices.

Place one slice of bread on the base of the tin, trimming it to fit. Place a slice of bread on either side of the inside of the tin and cut slices to fit both ends of the tin.

Spoon a little juice from the cooked berries onto the base to make sure that all the bread is uniformly soaked in juice. Add the fruit gradually, making sure the bread soaks up all the juices and turns red. When the tin is full of fruit, top with another slice of bread to seal it. Spoon over a couple of tablespoonfuls of juice from the berries that are left in the pan. You should have about half the amount of fruit left over to serve alongside each slice. Place in a bowl, cover with cling film and store in the fridge overnight.

Cover the top of the tin with cling film and place the pudding in the fridge overnight. Place a weight, such as a tin of baked beans, on top of the pudding to press it down. This will ensure that the mixture soaks into the bread and the pudding is firm enough to cut.

To turn out, peel back the cling film, then turn the pudding upside down onto a platter. Cut into slices and serve with the remaining berries and juice and a scoop of vanilla ice cream.

SERVES
8

LIMONCELLO LEMON TART WITH BLUEBERRY COMPOTE

I first discovered limoncello on a trip to the Amalfi coast in Italy. Since then, I always find an excuse to add a drop to any lemon dessert at the cookery school, as it really intensifies the lemon flavour.

INGREDIENTS

250g plain flour, plus extra for dusting

110g butter, chilled and cut into small cubes, plus extra for greasing

75g icing sugar

3 free-range egg yolks

1 free-range egg, lightly beaten

For the filling:

5 free-range eggs

160g caster sugar

2 tbsp finely grated lemon zest

225ml freshly squeezed lemon juice (about 3 lemons)

25ml limoncello liqueur

150ml double cream

1 tsp vanilla extract

For the blueberry compote:

2 punnets of blueberries

2 tbsp caster sugar

1 tbsp limoncello liqueur

1 tbsp water

Preheat the oven to 200°C/180°C fan/gas mark 6.

Place the flour and butter in a food processor and blitz to fine breadcrumbs.

Add the icing sugar and pulse to combine.

Add the egg yolks and pulse until it comes together. Do not overwork it as this makes the pastry tough.

Add a little ice-cold water if the pastry won't come together — just enough so that it will form a ball if you press it together.

Turn the mix onto a work surface. Form a ball with the mix, flatten it into a disc shape and wrap it in cling film. Chill for 60 minutes.

Brush a 24cm loose-bottomed tin with melted butter and dust lightly with flour, knocking off any excess flour.

Remove the pastry from the fridge and allow it to reach room temperature. Roll out the pastry and line the tin with it, pressing gently into the corners. Leave a slight overhang.

Cover the tin loosely with cling film and chill for 30 minutes.

Remove the tin from the fridge, prick the pastry base lightly with a fork (make sure you do not pierce the pastry), then line with baking parchment and baking beans and bake for 15–20 minutes. Remove the tin from the oven and remove the beans and parchment. Brush the pastry lightly with beaten egg and return to the oven for 25 minutes or until it is a light golden-brown. Remove from the oven and allow it to cool. When cool, trim off the edges neatly.

For the filling beat the eggs, sugar, lemon zest, lemon juice and limoncello in a bowl until well mixed. Add the cream and vanilla extract and mix well. Pour the mix into a measuring jug.

Reduce the oven to 180°C/160°C fan/gas mark 4.

Place the pastry case in its tin onto a baking tray and then place on the oven shelf. Carefully pour the filling into the pastry case until it comes to just below the top of the pastry shell.

Bake for about 25 minutes until set. The filling should have a slight wobble in the middle.

Remove and allow to cool completely before carefully removing from the tin.

To make the compote, place one punnet of blueberries in a small pot with the sugar, limoncello and water. Place on a high heat and bring to the boil.

Once boiling point is reached, reduce the heat to medium and allow the blueberries to gently cook until they begin to burst.

Remove the pot from the heat, stir in the second punnet of blueberries and set aside to cool.

Slice the tart and serve with the compote.

SERVES
6

VANILLA PANNA COTTA, FRESH BLACKBERRIES & A BLACKBERRY SOUP

Oftentimes the panna cotta that you get in restaurants is set with so much gelatine that it resembles a hockey puck. It should be lightly set and melt immediately in your mouth. To get the perfect set, this needs to be made the night before. I often serve this with the lemon madeleines on page 248.

INGREDIENTS

600ml cream

50g caster sugar

1 vanilla pod, with a small cut in one end

2 leaves of gelatine

2 punnets of blackberries

50ml water

50g + 1 tbsp icing sugar

fresh mint sprigs, to decorate

Place the cream, caster sugar and vanilla pod in a pot and gently bring to a simmer.

Place the gelatine in a bowl of cold water to soften for about 5 minutes, then squeeze out the excess water and add the leaves to the cream. Stir to dissolve.

Divide the mix between six lightly oiled dariole moulds and chill overnight.

To make the blackberry soup, cut the blackberries from one punnet in half lengthways. Place in a heatproof glass bowl and mix with the water and 50g of icing sugar. Cover the bowl with cling film and place over a pan of barely simmering water (a bain marie), making sure the bottom of the bowl doesn't touch the water. Bring the water to the boil, then reduce to a gentle simmer and let the blackberries cook for 1 hour. The cling film will puff up into a dome, but don't worry about that.

Remove the pan from the heat and strain the fruit through a fine sieve, collecting the juices in a clean bowl. Don't crush the fruit, as this will cloud the juices. (You can freeze the fruit until the next time you make a compote, when you can add them to the pot.) Leave the juices to cool and chill until required.

Place the second punnet of blackberries in a bowl, add the remaining tablespoon of icing sugar and stir gently to coat the berries. Stir again after 30 minutes and set aside until required.

Carefully unmould each panna cotta and place in the centre of a wide-brimmed soup plate. Pour the blackberry soup into the bowls around the panna cotta. Arrange some of the macerated berries on top and decorate with a fresh mint sprig.

LEMON & RASPBERRY PAVLOVA WITH WHITE CHOCOLATE & FRESH RASPBERRIES

There does seem to be a lot going on with this dessert, but the combination of flavours is deliciously vibrant and the addition of the white chocolate with the crispness of the pavlova adds a great crunch.

INGREDIENTS

4 egg whites, at room temperature

250g caster sugar

1 tsp cornflour

1 tsp white wine vinegar

1 tsp vanilla extract

50g good-quality white chocolate

2 tbsp lemon curd (page 50)

350ml double cream

500g fresh raspberries

fresh mint sprigs, to decorate

icing sugar, to dust

Preheat the oven to 150°C/130°C fan/gas mark 2. Line a large baking tray with non-stick baking paper.

Place the egg whites and 1 teaspoon of the sugar in a spotlessly clean, dry bowl. Whisk the egg whites until stiff peaks form. This means that when you turn off the mixer and quickly pull the beaters out of the mix and turn them upside down, the egg white peaks will stand up straight. This will take a couple of minutes, but be careful not to over beat the egg whites. The sign that you have over beaten is that the egg whites will begin to split and you will see water gathering in the bottom of your bowl. If this happens, you will have to start again.

Beat the rest of the sugar into the egg whites roughly one-third at a time, making sure the sugar is well incorporated into the egg whites after each addition. The egg whites will now be firm, shiny and glossy.

Sift in the cornflour, add the vinegar and vanilla extract and again beat well.

Transfer the mix to the centre of the lined baking tray and spread it out to the size of a large dinner plate. Bake in the centre of the oven for 1 hour. The pavlova should be lightly golden and crisp.

Turn off the oven, open the door slightly and allow the pavlova to cool completely, still in the oven. The pavlova will sink down and crack a little, but that is as it should be. When completely cool, remove from the oven and place on a serving plate.

Melt the white chocolate in a heatproof bowl set over a pan of barely simmering water (a bain marie), making sure the water doesn't touch the bottom of the bowl. Set aside until it's cool to touch but still liquid. Carefully spread the melted white chocolate over the top of the pavlova and leave to set.

Spread the lemon curd over the white chocolate.

Whip the cream to a consistency that will spread, then spread this neatly on top of the pavlova. Sprinkle the fresh raspberries over the top and decorate with a fresh mint sprig and a dusting of icing sugar.

INDEX